QUERY
CRAFT

Query Craft: The Writer-in-the-Know Guide to Getting Your Manuscript Requested

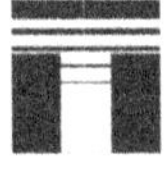

Published by Traderscape Publishing.

Edited by Warren Hammond
Art and design by Angie Hodapp

Paperback ISBN: 978-1-7349102-0-9
Ebook ISBN: 978-1-7349102-1-6

QUERY **CRAFT**

THE **WRITER-IN-THE-KNOW GUIDE**
TO GETTING YOUR MANUSCRIPT REQUESTED

ANGIE HODAPP

CONTENTS

INTRODUCTION

If your goal as a novelist is to secure the representation of a literary agent, then chances are you'll need to write a query letter. Of course, you probably already know that or you wouldn't have picked up a copy of this book!

Sure, there are other ways to get an agent's attention. Maybe you know someone in the industry (a published author, an acquiring editor, your neighbor's cousin's daughter's BFF who just landed a summer internship at Big Fancy Literary Agency) who can help you get your foot in an agent's door. (Figuratively speaking, that is, as showing up unannounced at a literary agent's door is rarely a good idea.) Or maybe you've mastered the face-to-face pitch, so you're making the rounds on the conference circuit. You're buying up pitch appointments and staking out the hotel bar, hoping Mx. Dream Agent stops by so you can buy them a drink and tell them about your manuscript…all of which can take quite a toll on your bank account.

So, yes, there are other roads you can travel, but a great majority of authors who have gained an agent's representation buckled down and learned how to write a good query letter. They sent that query letter out, received rejections (dozens, hundreds, more), thickened their skin, refined their query letter, sent it out again, revised their query letter again, kept sending it out, and persevered until at last they got a *yes*.

The pursuit of that *yes* is probably why you're reading this book. Which is good because helping you get that *yes* is why I wrote it.

This book is based on my many years of experience reading thousands upon thousands of query letters for the agent team at Nelson Literary Agency. It's also based on what I've learned from workshopping with the students in my query-writing classes over the years. What I will teach you in this book is not only how to craft a stellar query letter, but also how to avoid dozens of pitfalls and missteps that cause agents to dismiss so many queries after spending mere seconds scanning their content.

The path to *yes* is often lined with rejections. My hope is to make your path as short as possible.

WHO IS THIS BOOK FOR?

This book is for fiction writers who have completed a novel-length manuscript of ready-to-publish quality (or close to it) and are ready to seek the representation of a literary agent. It's for any fiction writer who wants to apply for the job of Professional Writer and sell their novels to publishing houses. It's also for writers who aren't that far along yet but know they someday will be. It's always a good time, and never too early, to familiarize yourself with the nuts and bolts of the publishing industry, especially given how quickly the industry changes.

In this book, you'll also find some tips on improving your story craft. This is because crafting a good pitch is entwined with crafting a good book. If you find that writing your pitch is more agonizing than it should be—more specifically, that you're having a hard time working one of the query-pitch elements I discuss in later chapters into your pitch—the problem might lie in the content or structure of your manuscript.

This book does not, however, offer much to writers looking for information on self- or independent-publishing, marketing, publicity, or the like, nor will it offer much substance to writers of poetry, short stories, scripts, or nonfiction. My query expertise comes from my years spent reading the slush piles (the term for unsolicited submissions, including queries) of agents working in the commercial, book-length fiction space, so if that's where your work fits, welcome to the roller coaster. Buckle up!

CHAPTER 1

QUERY BASICS

WHAT IS A QUERY LETTER?

PUT SIMPLY, A QUERY LETTER IS A ONE-PAGE BUSINESS letter that introduces you and your completed novel to the literary agents you are hoping will represent you, or to the editors you are hoping will acquire your work (if such editors work for publishing houses that don't require their authors to have an agent's representation).

Let's break that down a bit.

Your query letter should be professional in both tone and format, and, if printed out, it should fit on one letter-sized sheet of paper. Most querying happens via email nowadays, so printing your query isn't something you'll actually do unless you want to test its length. Instead, look at how your query fits on a computer screen and make sure the slush reader doesn't have to scroll down much, if at all, to read it in its entirety.

Your query letter sells your book. It should make agents lean forward in their chairs and shout, "I can't wait to read this!"

Better yet, "I can sell this!"

A well-crafted query pitch travels with your novel. It sells your prospective agent on your writing skills and story idea. Your agent will then use your pitch to get acquiring editors interested. Acquiring editors who want to extend you an offer will use your pitch to get their editorial directors or publishers to approve that offer. As soon as your book has a set publication date, your publisher's sales, marketing, and publicity teams will use your pitch to sell your book to subrights licensors, booksellers, librarians, and, most importantly, readers.

And it doesn't end there. You yourself will use your pitch when you're sitting behind an autograph table at a book store, conference, or convention, and a prospective reader stops to ask, "What's your book about?"

Stop thinking of writing a query pitch as a necessary evil and start thinking of it as the vital sales tool it actually is.

DO YOU NEED A LITERARY AGENT?

Before you start stressing yourself out over composing the perfect query letter (which, let me just say now, doesn't exist), please ask yourself: *Do I need a literary agent?*

I've met many writers in my classes at various conferences who are preparing to query, but they don't really understand why. They only know that they've finished a manuscript, and they're moving forward with the vague idea that querying is what they're supposed to do next. They know that signing with an agent is somewhat of a badge of honor within their writing communities. They know that their writing communities are often subtly sorted, though perhaps few will admit it out loud, into Agented and Not Agented (as well as Published and Not Published, and Self-Published and Traditionally Published, etc.). They know that "Agented" is a status they'd like to achieve.

The truth is, there are so many paths to publication available to writers today. Depending on your goals, the types of books you write, and the readership you are hoping to reach, you might not even need an agent. Or maybe you do. Or maybe you sign with an agent only to realize that you're more of an independently minded author who wants to do things your own way. Whatever the case, think of querying as the equivalent of applying for a job.

QUERY LETTERS ARE JOB APPLICATIONS.

Whether you're querying publishers directly or querying agents you hope will represent you, when you send a query letter, you are applying for the job of Professional Writer.

Consider what you already know about job-hunting. Anytime you apply for a job, it's best if you do your research before you write your cover letter or show up for your interview. You increase your chances of landing the job if you know three things: (1) what the job entails, (2) what niche the company fills within the scope of its particular industry, and (3) what the industry at large is all about.

So let's circle back to the original question: *Do I need a literary agent?*

The answer is…it depends. If you're not sure what literary agents do for their author-clients or how the behemoth that is the traditional-publishing industry works, then I encourage you to do a little more research before you begin querying.

Know about the job for which you are applying.

Know what niche the publisher or literary agent you're querying seeks to fill.

Know how traditional publishing works.

To learn more, please check my book *Do You Need a Literary Agent?: The Writer-in-the-Know Guide to a Literary Agent's Role in the Publishing Industry.*

QUERYING IS STRESSFUL. DO IT ANYWAY.

Still with me? Still ready to conquer the query? Awesome!

I want to take a second to acknowledge that there's a whole mess of stress surrounding the query process. And why wouldn't there be? Not only are you supposed to boil your 90,000-or-so-word novel down into a pithy pitch, but your pitch must be so evocative that it makes agents beg for your manuscript. Failure to elicit this response will get you a form rejection. Or, if you're lucky, a vague sentence or two about why the agent "didn't fall in love" with your premise, "didn't connect" with your characters, or "didn't get that must-have feeling" when they read your pitch. If you're trying to launch your writing career, the stakes never feel quite as high as they do when you're in the thick of the query process.

So what can you do?

Query anyway.

Accept that the best path forward is not *around* but *through.*

Accept that writing a really good attention-catching query pitch will be difficult.

Accept that the submissions process is work, and that you'll have to start treating it as a job.

Accept that you're going to get rejections and that rejections are not personal. Refuse to give rejections the power to define your work or your future as a writer.

Accept that querying, at least for now, is pretty much how the industry works. There are no reliable shortcuts on the slog through the slush pile.

Query anyway.

IT ALL STARTS WITH WRITING A GOOD BOOK.

On one hand, maybe you wrote the most amazing, groundbreaking novel your genre has ever seen. If you can't hack the query letter, that novel might never get requested or read.

On the other hand, maybe you crafted the most intriguing, evocative query letter in the world. If your manuscript isn't well executed, you're still going to get a rejection.

I've worked with quite a few writers who are convinced that their mounting pile of pink slips is due to an issue with their query letter. "Where does my query go wrong?" they ask in despair.

"Is it getting you requests for your full manuscript?" I ask.

"Yes! But I'm still getting rejections!"

The obvious response is that the problem lies not in your query, but in your manuscript. That's a bitter pill to swallow. A one-page letter (or, more specifically, a two-to-three-paragraph pitch) is easier to revise than a 90,000-word novel, yet the novel is often where the writer needs to focus their revision efforts.

If you get nothing else from this book, please tune in when I say success starts with writing a good book. Learning to do that takes patience and time. Apprentice yourself to the craft of fiction, and make sure your expectations are realistic.

WRITE YOUR QUERY FIRST.

Plenty of writers wait until they have a completed manuscript before they attempt to craft a query for it. It makes sense, right? Don't put the cart before the horse. Write the book before you try to sell it.

Is this good advice? Maybe. But maybe not. It depends on what kind of writer you are and how you get your novels done. Maybe you plot your novels first and generally stick to the plan as you write. Or maybe you write by the seat of your pants, sitting down each day with little or no idea what's going to happen on the page, and you write several drafts before you have a polished and ready-to-submit manuscript.

Either way, if you're a writer who wants to build a career in writing commercial fiction, then I strongly advise you to write a query pitch for every book idea that occurs to you. Keep a file of pitches for books you might write someday. Such a practice is extremely valuable.

First, it helps you take a 30,000-foot view of your story ideas. Are they exciting, or are you having a hard time making them sound anything other than quiet or ho-hum? Do they offer your intended audience a mix of familiar, recognizable tropes while at the same time adding something new—a unique twist, a different perspective—to the constantly evolving canon of your genre? Or do they sound too similar to other already-published works?

Second, it helps you zero in on your book's movie-trailer moments, those high emotional turning points in your plot (as you imagine your plot might look at this early stage) that will sell your book and keep readers turning pages.

Third, if after you write the pitch you decide to write the manuscript, then having the pitch sitting on your desk or pinned to the wall gives you something to return to when your story starts getting lost in the weeds—usually somewhere between 10,000 and 20,000 words.

Fourth, if you keep a file of thoughtfully crafted story pitches, you never have an excuse not to be writing, not to start something new.

Fifth, when you *do* sign with an agent and the agent asks you for five ideas for your next project so they can steer you toward the one they think would be most worth the next few months to a year of your writing life, *boom!* You're on the ball.

Few things are worse than completing a manuscript

and then realizing when you sit down to write the query pitch that not much really *happens* in your story. You can't even make the darned thing sound exciting to *yourself*. That does happen, and this might be the very best reason that writing your query first is a worthwhile practice.

ARE AGENTS REALLY JUST LOOKING FOR REASONS TO REJECT YOU?

"Agents are just looking for a reason to reject you." I hear this a lot where writers gather. Sometimes it's said by writers on panels at conferences or conventions to audiences of wide-eyed newbies. The panelists mean well, but the message is, "Your query had better be solid-gold perfect, or it's straight into the trash with you, and you will never ever in a million years get published!"

Cringe. What a terrifying and damaging message to send new writers.

Other times, it's stated by writers so worn down and jaded by rejection that, to feel better about their own efforts, they need others to feel the sting as well. For these writers, their own rejections couldn't possibly be the result of a sloppily written query, a derivative premise, or poorly executed sample pages. Instead, these writers comfort themselves with the notion that rejection is the result of agents *looking too closely* for tiny, inconsequential mistakes, or *not looking closely enough* past what they themselves consider minor query-letter missteps to the brilliant manuscript beyond, which is sure to become a bestseller. For these writers, guidelines and standards are petty, arbitrary hoops set up for them by publishing professionals (those reviled gatekeepers!) to jump through on their otherwise clear path to literary fame.

Again, cringe. This is head trash I encourage you to kick to the curb.

My response to "agents are just looking for a reason to reject you" is…

Yes and no.

First, let's look at the yes. As I said, we get something like 25,000 queries per year. Some agencies get more, some fewer. The bottom line is, more fiction is being written than can be published through traditional channels in a hundred-thousand lifetimes.

Okay, a hundred-thousand lifetimes might be a bit hyperbolic. The point is—and this is not meant to be discouraging; it's simply the product of logic and reason—not every writer is going to make the cut.

The economy of traditional print publishing is not a mystery. Bookstores and libraries know how many books they sell or check out to readers each year. This dictates how many books they will order annually from publishers and wholesalers. This, in turn, dictates how many new titles publishers will allow their acquiring editors to buy each year. And this dictates publishers' budgets, which dictates the advances they can offer authors, both new and established.

What about electronic publishing?

In the digital space, hundreds of thousands of new titles are being electronically published each year by both traditional houses and self-published writers. Independent publishing has shifted the question of *will my book be published?* (because of course it will, if you want it to) to *will my book make a profit?*

The chances of a digital-only release breaking out or even gaining respectable leverage in such a vast field of choices is slim. This, too, plays into the choices that agents and publishers make about which projects to represent or acquire.

So yes, agents have to make decisions about which projects to pursue. That's, in fact, one of the major things literary agencies exist to do.

Therefore, for slush readers, filters exist, and they must be applied.

So instead of thinking, "Agents are looking for a reason to reject me," think, "Agents are applying filters to my query letter as they read it, so I'll increase my chances of getting a close read if I learn what those filters are and avoid making the common mistakes that clog their filtration systems."

Now let's look at my no, which I hope is more resounding than my yes. No to the negative connotations of the tired adage "agents are just looking for a reason to reject you." No to the implication that agents stand at the Magical Gate of Publication, cackling and twirling their villainous mustaches as they soullessly fling brilliant works of heartbreaking genius into the burn barrel.

The truth is, if agents don't find manuscripts to sell, they don't make a living. Finding those brilliant works of genius is how they buy groceries and pay their mortgages and get their cars fixed and feed their pets and clothe their children. Agents are people, too, and their professional reputations and successes depend on their abilities to attract, recognize, compete for, and help develop the Next Big Thing.

In my opinion, the better axiom is "agents are looking for reasons to *represent* you." With every new query an agent opens, they're hoping to find a diamond—even a diamond in the rough.

WHAT ARE THE ODDS?

"How many query letters does your agency get?" This is a question I can count on getting in every query workshop I teach. I know that what my students are really asking is this: "What are the odds that my query will get pulled out of the slush pile?"

And I know that what they really want to know is, "What are my odds of getting published?"

So okay. Let's look at the numbers.

If the "how many queries" question were posed to me right now, at the time of this writing, I'd answer with a pretty solid estimate: I'd say that last year, we received approximately 25,000 queries. This works out to several hundred per week.

Of those 25,000 queries, approximately 670, or 2.68%, resulted in our request to see a full manuscript.

Of those 670 manuscripts, we offered representation on maybe two dozen. Several of those had offers from more than one agent, so not all of them signed with our agency.

So now we're looking at odds of one in 1,000, or around 0.1%. When writers hear this, their faces fall. Their shoulders slump.

"But wait!" I say. "It gets worse!"

Of the manuscripts we did sign, only a handful were acquired by editors at Big Five publishers. (Big Five refers to the five largest publishers in the US and their many imprints: Penguin Random House, Hachette, HarperCollins, Macmillan, and Simon & Schuster.) Just because you secured an agent's representation doesn't mean you're going to get published. Agents get rejected, too, when they submit their clients' manuscripts to editors. Plenty of manuscripts represented by agents never get acquired by an editor, never get published.

Not only that, but at the time of this writing, the agent field is crowded. A lot of new agents are hanging out their shingles, and they're signing a lot of new authors—but that doesn't mean publishers are acquiring more books. So your offer of representation, while certainly something to celebrate, is only the beginning of another round of revisions, submissions, and, possibly, tough-to-swallow rejections.

Now the light in those writers' eyes dims and threatens to go out. All hope is lost. Why carry on?

"But wait!" I say. "It's not as dire as you think!"

First, one agency's statistics are not the same as any other agency's statistics. Stats like this are always anecdotal, useful only insofar as we look at what's *behind* the numbers. Which we'll do here in a bit.

Second, much of what agents see in their slush piles is, to be brutally honest, easily dismissible. Beyond the naiveté of newer writers who mean well but simply aren't ready for publication, unprofessionalism abounds. We'll get into specifics on that later, too, but for now, imagine the literary equivalent of job candidates who show up for their interviews chomping gum, wearing ripped jeans and flip-flops, armed with a battery of explanations for why getting fired from their last three jobs wasn't their fault. Perhaps such candidates don't really want the job they're interviewing for, or perhaps they simply think their strategy is solid. Either way, they're stepping on their own feet.

That means that writers like you who take the time to learn how to craft a professional query letter that contains an evocative pitch are already head and shoulders above your competition. You're already well-positioned to rise to the top of the slush pile.

Finally, while it may or may not be useful to you to think in terms of numbers, odds, and statistics, the only figure that really matters in this industry is this: *100% of novels that don't get finished don't get published.* So take out the head trash, tune out the industry noise, and *write.* Buckle down and finish your book to the best of your abilities. Then start—and *finish*—your next book. And your next after that. Solicit feedback. Be open to listening and learning from what others say about your writing. Hone your craft. Be aware of the specific ways in which, with each book, you're becoming a better writer. Remember: It all starts with writing a good book.

CHAPTER 2

THE ANATOMY OF AN AGENT'S SLUSH PILE

When writers hear how many queries agents receive per week, per month, per year, they tend to assume they are jumping into an overcrowded pool in which everyone is an equally strong swimmer.

Not true.

What follows is, admittedly, a simplified and anecdotal breakdown of what we might reasonably assume appears in a typical slush pile. Other agencies' mileages may vary. Regardless, I do think it's useful for querying writers to understand what agents and their readers encounter when they sit down to read what's in their inboxes.

For this section, imagine one of those Punnett squares you learned about in the genetics unit of high-school biology: a grid with two rows and two columns. The columns are *Faulty Story* and *Good Story*. The rows are *Poorly Executed* and *Well Executed*. The percentages in each quadrant of our Punnett square are what we'll discuss next as we look at each cell in turn.

<table>
<tr><th></th><th>Faulty Story</th><th colspan="2">Good Story</th></tr>
<tr><td>Poorly Executed</td><td>20%</td><td colspan="2">30%</td></tr>
<tr><td>Well Executed</td><td>30%</td><td>10%</td><td>10%</td></tr>
</table>

FAULTY STORIES POORLY EXECUTED

I'd estimate that some 20% of submissions fall into the first quadrant. These are submitted by new writers—writers who might have some inkling of what they're doing but who have most likely been working in solitude, away from the beneficial influences of critique groups, beta readers, writing conferences, and craft workshops. Some of these writers mention older novels as comparable titles, indicating they aren't up to speed on what readers of their genre are currently demanding. Frankly, these writers don't know what they don't know, and I commend them for putting themselves and their work out there. But they are not yet ready for the job of Professional Writer.

If you think this is you, slow down. Recognize that you're not ready. Precious few creative professionals got to the top of their game on their first try, despite our society's obsession with the lone-wolf archetype and the overnight-success story. Focus on improving your manuscript by learning command of the English language and how to craft a compelling story. Take classes and workshops. Find a critique group. Apprentice yourself to a master. Ask trusted beta readers—people who are not related to you—to tell you where your prose, execution, and story craft are working, and more importantly where they're going wrong.

GOOD STORIES POORLY EXECUTED

In the next quadrant to the right are the submissions I'd estimate make up some 30% of our slush pile. These submissions present promising story ideas, but the execution demonstrated either in the writing of the query letter itself or in the accompanying sample pages just isn't up to snuff. If this is you, you might be getting requests for your full manuscript, but those requests aren't turning into offers of representation. Your manuscript isn't closing the deal.

This is where an agent's rejection letter might say something like, "Great concept, but the writing just isn't there yet," or, "After reading the first fifty pages, I was still waiting for the story to start." You can't hide average or below-average writing (prose, mechanics) or loose story craft (pacing, structure) behind a unique concept or a well-crafted pitch. As before, take some classes and workshops, find a critique group or a few trusted beta readers, and open yourself up to seeking and incorporating feedback.

FAULTY STORIES WELL EXECUTED

I'm going to estimate that another 30% of our slush pile falls into the bottom left quadrant of our grid. This is where an agent's response might be, "Great writing, but I just didn't fall in love with the story or characters like I hoped I would," or, "You're a strong writer, but I'm not sure the story will stand out in the current market." They might even come right out and say that your story feels derivative, that it doesn't feel fresh or unique.

Whatever the case, keep in mind that "faulty story" is highly subjective. If you can write compelling prose that demonstrates mastery of the language (skills that are rarer than you might think), then an agent or editor might be willing to take you on and work with you to revise the story itself. They might be more likely to say, "The story's a mess, but dang, this author can *write*!" In other words, we can coach the *craft* of writing, but we can't coach the *art* of writing. Helping a writer improve their story's structure and execution is doable, if the writer is open to such coaching, but if the art isn't there—if there's no compelling voice, no masterful use of language, no clear, illuminating turns of phrase—well, that's harder.

In any case, your odds of getting an agent to take a chance on you are better in this space than in the "good story poorly executed" space, especially if the agent is newer and actively building their list. It happens. It's out of the ordinary, and you shouldn't wait around hoping it happens to you. Instead, focus on what you can control, which is honing your storytelling skills.

GOOD STORIES WELL EXECUTED

This final bottom-right quadrant, good stories well executed, makes up the final 20% of our slush pile. This where you want to be. However, there's one more element to consider here, and it's a big one: marketability. So we're going to split this quadrant in half. This means we can estimate that 10% of good stories well executed are marketable (they are well-timed for the current market, given editors' and readers' shifting tastes in a particular genre) and 10%, sadly, aren't.

The unmarketable submissions are real heartbreakers among agents, and your query letter for such a submission may or may not elicit an offer of representation. It all comes down to what we mean when we say unmarketable.

For some agents, unmarketable means, "I'm not the right agent to take this out into the market." Maybe the agent recognizes the literary quality of the work, but they just don't know the right editor to send it to. Or maybe the agent expects that the manuscript will sell, but they simply aren't connecting with it deeply enough to be its best champion—and, by extension, *your* best champion.

Why does that matter?

Think of the latest literary smash that every member of your book club raved about, but for whatever reason it just didn't appeal to you. That happens to agents, too. And you want an agent who loves your work and shares your literary vision. After all, they're the ones who will be representing you in face-to-face conversations with acquiring editors, booksellers, librarians, foreign-rights agents and editors, and movie/TV agents and producers. No way an agent who feels dispassionately about your manuscript, who views it as a mere commodity, is going to come across to others in the industry as genuinely thrilled to be representing it. An agent's gut feeling about your work matters to your career, and it will affect your long-term success.

In other situations, unmarketable might mean that editors right now aren't buying books similar to yours. Remember not so long ago when vampires and dystopias were anathema to acquiring editors and, therefore, agents? In publishing, which, admittedly, operates at the speed of molasses in January, by the time a trend becomes recognizable on bookstore shelves, editors are already over it. The manuscripts editors are buying today won't be available to readers for 18 to 24 months. This is why trend-chasing is not a recommended method of building a writing career, unless, of course, you (1) write extremely fast, (2) craft extremely well, and (3) deliver the tropes of the trending genre or subgenre both reliably and consistently in a way that feels fresh to readers. But rare is the writer who can do all three.

Finally, unmarketable might mean that what you've written doesn't fit inside any recognizable literary box. I get that the idea of literary boxes (i.e., genres) can be constraining, even unfair. But if an agent doesn't know how to categorize or talk about your book, they will have a hard time selling it to an editor. If an editor doesn't know how to categorize or talk about your book, they will have a hard time convincing their publishers to approve its acquisition. The publisher's sales team will have a hard time talking about your book to booksellers and librarians, and booksellers and librarians will have a hard time talking about your book to readers. Genre is not a dirty word, but a useful way to help book-industry folks get your book into the hands of its appropriate readership.

Publishing is a business, so remember how many hearts and minds your book has to pass through before it makes it into the hands of someone willing to trade their hard-earned money to own a copy of it.

While some aspiring writers decry the pressure they feel to write neatly categorizable fiction (many because they are certain their ideas defy conventional genres), knowing that difficult-to-describe or hard-to-categorize books can so easily get derailed at any stop along the path to publication might encourage them to embrace writing for audiences of particular genres. Fair or not, I do tend to recommend that writers who are trying to break into publishing for the first time stick to conventions. Your ability to deliver familiar genre tropes (with your own unique style, world, characters, and voice, of course) within acceptable word-count ranges can be the very thing that gets your foot in the door. After you secure that first contract, be a team player and make your deadlines. Show that you're up to the job of Professional Writer. Exceed expectations. Then, once you have some ears to bend, float your less-conventional ideas past your publishing partners. Debut authors are risks, but once you're a known quantity, you're a lot more likely to get the green light to dive into those out-of-the-box novels you've been dying to write.

In any case, unmarketable today might turn into "perfect for the market" in a year or two. If an agent signs on to represent you, and then takes your book out on submission and it doesn't sell, what is the first thing they're going to say to you? Probably "what's next?" or "what else do you have?" or "get started on something new."

Don't stop writing.

Being out on submission can turn even the most calm, levelheaded writer into a bundle of raw, sparking, white-hot nerves. Use those nerves to fuel your next manuscript. Always have something new in the hopper.

If your submission is among that final 10% in the bottom right corner of our Punnett square—a good story both well executed and well timed for the current market—then you're off to the races. These are the submissions that get a quick offer of representation, if not several.

If you're still ready to charge ahead with your query letter even if the road gets rocky and discouraging, then let's move on. Next up: query prep work!

CHAPTER 3

BEFORE YOU QUERY

FINISH YOUR MANUSCRIPT

NOTE THAT I MENTIONED ABOVE THAT YOUR QUERY letter introduces your *completed* novel. Remember that if you are seeking your first agent or traditional-publishing deal, then you should be prepared, if your full manuscript is requested, to send it immediately.

Agents aren't interested in what you're working on or what idea you have that you swear you can turn into a completed manuscript in a few weeks or months. If an agent likes your query pitch enough to request your manuscript, then they want to read it *now*. You are hobbling yourself if you are unprepared to strike while the opportunity is hot. So wait until your novel is not only complete, but also revised and edited to the best of your abilities before you begin to query.

After your debut novel hits the market, your agent can sell your subsequent books based on synopses. But as a debut author, your break-in novel must be complete before you begin querying.

CREATE A TARGETED LIST OF AGENTS

Casting a wide net—that is, sending your query to every single agent listed in all the major agent directories—is a bad approach to querying. First, agents aren't in the business of finding clients for other agents, especially clients who can't be bothered in the first place to research which agents are appropriate for their book.

Second, this approach is a waste of your time. If you're writing personalized queries to every agent listed in the major directories, isn't that time you could have spent working on your next novel?

On the other hand, if you think you're saving time by sending out one mass email, CCing or BCCing hundreds of agents with your generic, non-personalized query letter, then you're shooting yourself in the aspirations. Mass emails are a quick reject for slush readers because they earmark you as someone who either doesn't understand the industry or is too self-important to be bothered with pesky details and guidelines.

Instead, create a targeted list of agents to query. Look for agents who (1) represent the type of book you've written and (2) are currently open to queries and actively seeking new clients. How do you do that? Start by searching these online agent directories:

- Publishers Marketplace, publishersmarketplace.com. This is the best place to look for agents who represent particular authors. This is also where you can check out an agent's recent sales, which is useful to know. With the exception of new agents who are building their client lists, an agent who hasn't sold a book in a while might be slowing down. Maybe they're nearing retirement, spending more time with their families, or transitioning to something other than active selling. How hard will that agent work to sell your book?
- Manuscript Wish List, manuscriptwishlist.com. This is where agents talk about what they wish would land in their inboxes. You can also follow #MSWL on Twitter.
- The Association of Authors' Representatives, aaronline.org. Members of this professional organization for literary agents are listed on this site. While there are legitimate reasons reputable agents might not be members of the AAR, it might matter to you that the agents you're querying are

members and are, therefore, beholden to the AAR's canon of ethics.

- Agent Query, agentquery.com. This is a decent site where you can search for agents who represent your genre.

Writer's Digest's *Writer's Market and Guide to Literary Agents* is worth a mention here as well, though the full menu of online features is only available to paid subscribers. This guide is published annually in print, too, and can be found at most book stores.

Finally, look at the acknowledgments in books that are similar to yours, written by authors whose readers you think would also enjoy your book. Most authors thank their agents in their acknowledgments, so look there to add a few more agents to your targeted list.

NOTE AGENTS' SUBMISSION GUIDELINES

Once you have a good list in front of you, visit the individual websites of each agent on your list. This is where you'll find the most trusted and up-to-date information about how to query them. Are they currently open to queries? Agents do close to queries now and then: during holidays, leading up to big trade events, whenever their responsibilities and obligations to their existing clients are piling up. Make sure your query will actually get read before you send it.

Check whether all the agents on your list represent your genre. Have I said that before? Yes. It's important!

Do they want you to send a query letter only, or do they want you to include sample pages? Do they say how long you can expect to wait for a response? Not all agents send responses to all the queries they receive; some simply indicate that no response equals a rejection. (Call me crazy, but that, in my humble opinion, is shockingly rude. Nobody seeking a professional relationship in a professional manner deserves to be left hanging.)

As you get deeper into the query process, keep your targeted-agent list updated. If you decide in the future to write something in a different genre, start a new agent list for that genre. Always note whom you queried, when you queried them, when you received a response, and what the response was. Don't be the flighty writer who sends those emails saying they can't remember if they already queried, or they're sorry they queried a second time because they remembered in the middle of the night that they queried last June and received a rejection.

Tracking your professional communications is part of the job of Professional Writer, so take it seriously.

PREPARE YOUR EMAIL ACCOUNT

Most querying is done via email or web-based form

these days. In fact, I don't know a single agent out there who still wants you to print your query out on a piece of paper, fold it, stuff it in an envelope, address it, stamp it, and walk it down to the local post office to drop it the collection slot.

At Nelson Literary Agency, we get a couple calls per month, give or take, from folks who don't have a computer or an email account and want to know how they can still query us. We stick firm (though as gently as possible) to the fact that we don't accept queries via snail mail. Then we advise them to visit their local libraries and have someone there help them set up a free email account.

Why aren't we more accommodating? Frankly, the prospect of working professionally in a technology-driven industry with someone who isn't set up to participate in regular, basic electronic communication is not attractive. Plus, how did these folks write their manuscripts? By hand? On a typewriter?

Querying happens online. Period. And until some newer, more-advanced technology comes along to replace the internet, the publishing industry will never slide back into the halcyon days of self-addressed stamped envelopes.

Given that, there's no small amount of hygiene that you should perform on your email account before you query.

First, your email account should be yours and yours alone. Tons of married couples still share one email address. But when we get a query from, say, ronaldandruthie@domain.com, it's a little off putting. Who's querying us: Ronald or Ruthie? Sure, I can scroll down and see whose name is at the bottom of the query—if the author remembered to include their name (you'd be surprised). But, frankly, using an email account you share with your spouse to conduct business-related communications is unprofessional. Not only that, but I've taken pitches at writing conferences over the years from women whose husbands don't know they write, or their husbands keep tabs on what they write and who they talk to online. When I see an email from a shared address come through, I don't know if it's a sweet, lovey thing or a controlling thing. Does Ronald know Ruthie writes? Do I have to go through Ronald to communicate with Ruthie about her writing? Use ronaldandruthie@domain.com for personal and family communications, but not to apply for the job of Professional Writer.

Second, it's also confusing when we get a query from ronaldsnead@domain.com, but it's signed Ruthie Snead. Even more confusing, it's signed Jerri Jacobs. Either this writer has a pen name, or they're borrowing a friend or family member's email account to query. Again, sign up for your own email address. It's fast, free, and easy.

Third, make your email address simple and professional: firstlast@domain.com is great, but sexxxybeeest69@domain.com is not. Generic nicknames or self-identifiers, like sci-fi-scribe, dragonwriter, mygoldenpen, words-R-life, or love2write are also not super professional. Stick with firstlast@domain.com or, if you already own your own domain, first@firstlast.com.

Fourth, set your "from" field to your first and last name. Whatever is entered in this field in your email account's settings is how you'll be listed in your recipient's inbox. A lot of people who use the email addresses that come free with their service-provider accounts don't know they have to go into their account settings and change the default in the "from" field. Therefore, we get a lot of queries from writers named CenturyLink Customer. Other email services use your email address as your default "from," which means you'll show up in the recipient's inbox as ruthiesnead@domain.com <ruthiesnead@domain.com> instead of as Ruthie Snead <ruthiesnead@domain.com>.

Fifth, if you're writing under a pen name and that's how you want to be known in your writing career, then own it. Set up an email address for that pen name and use that pen name to sign all queries and subsequent communications. The exception is if you are already an established author who has published novels under a different name, and now you wish to reinvent yourself or write in a new genre, and you're letting us know that. Then, of course, you'll want to mention your past publications and the name under which they were published.

Another exception is if your query letter mentions real-life professional accomplishments germane to your novel's subject matter—like maybe you're well known for something (say, museum security) relevant to your novel (which is about, say, a museum heist) and have a platform that could be leveraged to boost sales of your book. In any case, if you use a pen name, are offered representation, and wish to accept, then that's when you'll let your new agent know your full legal name, as that's what they'll use on all legal documents, including the agency agreement, tax forms, and publishing contracts.

Finally, make sure your email address is set up to receive replies. Earthlink used to have a nasty little anti-spam feature that blocked responses from anyone not in your Earthlink address book with an automatic reply that said something like "You are not an approved sender so please fill out this form to become an approved sender." If your email provider has a feature like this, then make sure you add the email addresses of all the agents you're querying to your address book or approved-sender list. I strongly advise you not to set up hoops an agent might need to jump through in order to communicate with you.

Now that you've done all your query prep work, let's

take a look at some common query letter pitfalls and how to avoid them.

CHAPTER 4

COMMON QUERY-LETTER PITFALLS AND HOW TO AVOID THEM

In general, I see a lot of writers make many of the same easily avoidable mistakes in their query letters. While none alone might lead to an automatic rejection, they do, cumulatively, raise an agent's little red flag. The more mistakes and missteps an agent sees, the higher their little red flag goes until eventually they stop reading your query and move on to the next. With that in mind, here is a quick run-down on what to avoid so your query doesn't get caught in an agent's filtration system.

THE QUERY IS TOO LONG OR TOO SHORT

As already mentioned, your query letter is a business letter that, if printed out, should fit on one letter-sized sheet of paper. Anything far longer or shorter than one printed page will push their little red flag higher up the pole. In later chapters, we'll dive deep into the four parts of a query letter and how long each part should be, but for now, know that most agents can tell as soon as they open your query if it's an appropriate length. Some writers give nothing more than a quick logline—a sentence or two that's more akin to the old elevator pitch made famous by the screenwriting industry. That's too short for a query letter. Others give a full-blown synopsis. That's too long. By the time you're done reading this book, you'll have a much better sense of a query letter's proper length.

THE GENRE OR WORD COUNT IS OFF

Queries for submissions that aren't right for the agent or for novels of problematic length are quick passes. In sum, you might get a quick-fire pass if any of the following apply.

- The agent doesn't represent the genre you specified in your query.
- The project's word count is too high or too low for a *novel*, for the *genre*, or for the intended *audience*. (We'll look more at word count in a bit.)
- Your query doesn't specify a genre or word count.
- The story you pitched in your query doesn't fit the genre you specified.

As already mentioned, you wouldn't believe how many writers think it's a good idea to query as many agents as possible, regardless of whether those agents represent their genre. They set out to query literally every agent listed on Publishers Marketplace or in the latest edition of *Guide to Literary Agents*. My sense is that this practice results from the "cast a wide net" networking mentality. However, the idea that "you don't represent what I write, but I'm going to query you anyway because maybe you know someone who does, and you're going to be so blown away by my work that you're going to hook me up" is, in fact, a bit silly.

Think of it this way: If you need a window replaced in your home, you don't start by calling plumbers, electricians, and painters, hoping that one of them might get so personally invested in the success of your window-installation project that they take time out of their workday to hook you up with the right window installer. ("Because surely you *know* some window installers who could help me, right?") Just no. Instead, you do your research. You Google window installers, then you narrow your search by looking at which of them specialize in your type of project, which work in your area, and which have earned good customer reviews.

Likewise, if you need an agent who represents middle-grade fantasy, you don't send your query to agents who don't list middle-grade fantasy on their websites as something they're looking to represent. You just don't.

Lots of agencies, Nelson Literary Agency included, are now accepting queries through QueryManager, an online submission tool tied to QueryTracker. (If you're serious about querying, I highly recommend you check out QueryTracker!) QueryManager goes a long way toward filtering out many of these submissions, which is awesome for slush readers because what a time saver! First, QM allows agents to build custom query forms that include a list of the genres and subgenres they're currently looking to represent. Because authors are required to select a genre for their project, those who don't see their genre listed on agent's query form realize (hopefully) that querying this agent is a waste of everyone's time.

However, I just read a query today for one of our agents from an author who wrote, "I didn't see a genre on your query form that matched the book I wrote, so I just picked one." This was likely a symptom of the writer not really understanding genre in general. For writers who do, if your genre isn't listed on the agent's form, then you should not query that agent.

Agents can also set custom word-count rules that will red-flag queries for manuscripts that are too long or too short. Yes, it literally tags such queries with a red flag icon. Queries for manuscripts with problematic word counts will still come through, but agents can sort their inboxes by word count and give the outliers a cursory glance before most likely sending a rejection.

We'll go deeper into genres and word counts later, but for now, understand that knowing your genre and getting your word count in line with that genre are important to keeping a slush reader's eyes on your query.

THE WRITER HASN'T DEMONSTRATED COMMAND OF THE LANGUAGE

You might be a master storyteller, with delightfully complex characters running around in your head begging to be next in your storytelling queue. But if you can't effectively and artfully communicate on the page, if you can't masterfully wield the tools of your craft (grammar, mechanics, syntax, semantics, and so on), you're not ready for the job of Professional Writer. That doesn't mean you won't be ready someday; you're just not ready now.

We get a handful of queries each week from writers whose first language is not English—or who, sadly, write as though it is not. A savvy slush reader can tell within a sentence or two by your word choice, phrasing, and mechanics whether you've achieved a basic command of written English. If you haven't, then slush readers won't make it to your pitch.

Some of these writers are published in other countries

and are trying to find an agent who will help them get their work translated into English and published in the United States. Note also that translation-to-English deals are not something our agency handles at this time, so for us, such a query would be quick pass. *Do your research.* If you don't, you'll get a quick pass, too.

That's not to say that your query has to be 100% perfect. A knockout query pitch with a misspelled word or misplaced comma isn't going to get an auto-reject. At least not from me; other slush readers or agents have different philosophies. For me, it's a universal truth that all writers need editors. I'm not expecting perfection, but I am expecting that someone applying for the job of Professional Writer is capable of demonstrating a higher-than-average command of written English. If after reading a one-page query letter I cringe at the thought of reading 80,000 more words written by that writer, then I'm going to send a rejection.

THE FORMATTING IS BAD

Poor formatting is another misstep that can lead an agent to quickly dismiss your query. Formatting is, in sum, how the ink looks on the page—or, nowadays, how the pixels look on the screen. Poor formatting leads to visual clutter that can detract from the content of your pitch.

- Is your query letter one giant, off-putting block

of text? Try adding some paragraph breaks… keeping in mind, of course, that paragraph breaks aren't arbitrary. They indicate transitions or shifts in topic. If you are unable to construct basic paragraphs, then you are not ready for the job of Professional Writer.

- Are you adding vertical space between paragraphs *and* indenting each paragraph's the first line? It should be one or the other, not both. Note that in online communication, as well as in written professional or business communication, block paragraphing is standard. That means separating paragraphs by vertical space only, keeping the first line of each paragraph flush left.
- Did you justify both margins, leading to some very gappy lines of text and some very tight ones? Switch over to left-justify (align-left) and leave the right margin ragged.
- Did you use a fancy font in larger- or smaller-than-usual size in any colors other than black? Did you sprinkle in lots of **bold**, *italics*, or ALL CAPS? Do your ellipses have more than three dots? Did you use lots of exclamation points? If yes, go back and clean all that up. It's messy and makes your query letter look more like a fifth-grader's book report than a business letter from professional writer.

THERE ARE IMAGES

Another major contributor to visual clutter is images. Your query is not where you include your author photo or a flashy little GIF. Nor is it where you insert the artwork you envision appearing on your book's cover or the sketches you want to appear at the beginning of each chapter. Your publisher will handle all the artwork associated with your book, and your agent will negotiate your level of involvement in that process. Hint: You will have little to no input. Therefore, any mention you make in your query letter regarding the art or production of your book earmarks you as someone who doesn't understand the industry you're applying to work in. Your query should do one thing and one thing alone: sell your manuscript. After that happens, you'll have a team of professionals making most of the decisions about how that manuscript becomes a book.

THERE ARE EXCESSIVE LINKS

If you have a website, whether it's related to your writing or to some other aspect of your life, it's OK to include a link in your signature block at the bottom of your query letter.

What you want to avoid is asking an agent to *click here for X, click here to read more about Y, click here to see Z.* This is most often done by writers trying to make a case for why their novel should be published. They've written a novel about some hot-button social issue or universally acknowledged hardship (say, human trafficking or caring for a loved one with Alzheimer's), and they want to educate the agent about how many people are affected by that issue or hardship, attempting to present a market before actually pitching their novel.

That in itself is not a great strategy—your pitch and the novel behind it should stand on their own without having to be propped up by facts and figures. But the bigger problem is that the whole function of a query letter is to encapsulate everything you want the agent to know about your novel *briefly and in one place*, so asking them to link to reading material external to your query is a wasted effort. Besides, no agent in the world has to be convinced that human-trafficking is a tragedy or that Alzheimer's is hell, so statistics about those affected aren't going to sell your manuscript. What *is* going to sell your manuscript is your hook, your mastery of your craft, your unique voice, and your complex characters with plights that evoke emotion. (There's a reason "you cry, you buy" is a saying among agents and editors.)

The biggest chunk of your query letter's real estate should be focused on your pitch. Keep your query focused on character and plot. (I'll show you how in later chapters of this book)

Another link-related mistake I've seen writers make is posting their query on their own website, and then sending agents a link to it. That's a quick reject because it makes you seem too self-important to be bothered with the pesky details of agents' submission guidelines. Following guidelines is part of being professional. Resist the urge to cut corners.

THERE ARE HEADINGS

Headings alone won't get you an auto-reject from me. But I do want to point out that it should be completely unnecessary to label the various parts of your query letter. I've seen tons of different headings and subheadings used in query letters, most commonly things like *Introduction, Synopsis, Pitch, About Me, Bio, Comparable Titles, Market Analysis, Intended Audience, Summary, Back Cover Copy,* and *Logline*, among others. A well-crafted query letter should be brief enough, and the information should flow naturally enough, that the reader should be 100% clear on what they're reading without the added clutter of headings.

THE DICTION IS ELEVATED

When a query letter opens with elevated diction—something like "I have penned a manuscript which I believe may be of particular interest to you given your stated literary tastes, though I fear that at present, my success at securing the services of a freelance editor notwithstanding, it is a bit of a lengthy tome"—my little red flag starts climbing. This is a writer who's trying too hard to sound smart. Trust me: You're better off sticking with clear, personable, contemporary-sounding diction. If I hear a nineteenth-century Brit in my head when I'm reading your query letter, then you'd better be submitting historical fiction—and even then, querying in the voice of your characters is a little too fancy and precious. It's risky, and I don't advise it.

Tuck these common query-letter missteps into your back pocket for now. Return to them later, after you read the next few chapters and write your query letter, to make sure you're still on the right path.

CHAPTER 5

THE FOUR-PART QUERY LETTER

PART ONE: THE GREETING

A TYPICAL ONE-PAGE QUERY LETTER IS MADE UP OF FOUR parts. They are (1) the greeting, which is optional, (2) the project summary, (3) the pitch, and (4) the bio. Master these parts, and you'll be well on your way to crafting a query letter that's clear, concise, and complete—and that gets your manuscript requested.

The greeting is optional, though many writers do choose to open their query letters with a brief greeting. *Brief* is the key word here. Remember, your entire query letter should, if printed out, fit on a single piece of paper. As such, your query letter's real estate is valuable, and the lion's share should be spent on your pitch. Don't waste too much time on the greeting. If you do include one, keep it not only brief, but also personal and professional.

In other words, the function of the greeting is to establish a quick connection with the agent you're querying. If no such connection exists, then it's fine to simply omit the greeting and begin with the project summary (part two).

What do I mean by connection? If you met this agent at a conference, heard them speak on a panel at a writing event, or took a class or workshop they taught, then it's OK to mention that in the greeting. If you are a regular reader of the agent's blog or newsletter, you can mention that here, too. If you have a friend or colleague in common, yep, mention it—especially if that friend or colleague is willing to provide you with a referral.

Another thing that's definitely worth mentioning is if you're a fan of an author this agent represents. This shows that you are familiar with the types of work this agent is excited about—you're not just shooting in the dark by sending them your submission.

In a lot of queries, the bio is combined in the project summary. We'll look at some examples in a bit. But first, here are some pitfalls to avoid in crafting your query letter's greeting.

FALSE REFERRALS

If the agent invited you to submit, or if you're submitting based on a referral, *definitely* mention that in the greeting. However, do be careful about claiming a referral that might not be a true referral. For example, if you ask a published writer if their agent is accepting queries right now, and they reply, "Yeah, you should totally send her your query," that's not a referral. Therefore, "Your author So-and-So recommended that I query you" is a stretched truth. Instead, opt for something like this: "I met your client So-and-So at Fancy Conference and they spoke highly of you."

Similarly, if an agent speaking on a panel extends a general invitation to the audience—something like, "I'm open to queries, so if anyone here today would like to query me, please do"—do *not* open your query letter with, "You invited me to submit to you." That's another stretched truth. Instead, opt for: "I attended your panel on Topic at Big Literary Event, where you mentioned you were open to queries. I enjoyed what you had to say and would love the opportunity to work with you."

A referral is only a referral if the person referring you contacts the agent on your behalf to talk up your skills as a writer and pave the way for your submission. Agents, like all humans, don't take kindly to being misled, so despite any temptation you might feel to gain an advantage in the slush pile, don't start your professional writing career off on the wrong foot.

GENERIC SALUTATIONS

"Dear Agent" is a surefire way to communicate to the recipient that you're cutting corners. Take the time to personalize each query letter. It matters. Likewise, "To Whom It May Concern" is dated, as are "Dear Sir" and "Dear Madam." These are not only shudderingly gendered, but they're so stiff and formal that they come off as elevated, like the author is trying too hard to impress. Stick with Dear First Last, Dear First, or Dear Mx. Last.

MISSPELLED OR INCORRECT NAMES

We get no small number of submissions from authors who *did* personalize their query letters…but then they did a cut-and-paste job and forgot to update the agent's name before hitting send. Likewise, it's mind-boggling how many writers misspell our agents' names. Kristin becomes Kristen. Nelson becomes Nielson or Nelsen or Nielsen. Danielle becomes Daniel. Joanna becomes JoAnne. And Quressa? Her name has been spelled in too many creative ways to count. Please pay attention to detail. Remember: You're applying for the job of Professional Writer. Spelling counts and details matter.

FLATTERY

As mentioned, it's fine to open your query letter with

a brief greeting that establishes a connection with the agent you're querying. But again, reserve your query's real estate for your pitch. Going on and on about how the recipient is your dream agent, or about how something they tweeted or said during a workshop changed your life, or about how impressed you are with their recent sales isn't doing you any favors. At the end of the day, the success of your query letter is going to come down to your pitch. Flattery isn't going to make up for a mediocre pitch, so save your space and energy for that.

SELF-DEPRECATION OR SELF-DOUBT

Many a query letter opens apologetically: "I don't really know how to write a query letter, but here goes," or, "I'm probably doing this wrong, but please read my submission anyway." This is not a solid strategy. If you don't have confidence in your work, or in your skills and potential as a Professional Writer, then you're not ready to query. An agent's first impression is formed by the tone of your query letter. If you lead with your weaknesses, we're going to believe you.

"THIS IS A SIMULTANEOUS SUBMISSION."

Here's another fossilized phrase from the olden days of paper-and-postage submissions. Back then, you submitted to one "Sir" at a time, and it was expected that you wait until you received an official rejection from Sir A before you submitted to Sir B—unless you offered this stock phrase as notification that your submission was out for consideration by other publishers. No longer. While this might still be an expectation of small presses or short-story markets, it has nothing to do with querying agents. Agents know you're querying widely. That's simply how it's done. So when you use this phrase in a query letter to an agent, you're demonstrating that you're behind the times.

"ACCORDING TO YOUR WEBSITE…"

This is a common way to open a query letter, but it's bland. It's mediocre. It's a throwaway phrase that wastes space. And all it communicates is that you visited the agent's website—which is important but should really go without saying. It's much stronger to establish a connection by mentioning a specific author or book the agent represents and why that author or book is an inroad to you and your book. Quoting the agent's website to them won't help you stand out in the slush pile; in fact, so many writers do it that it might actually make you blend in.

"I AM SEEKING REPRESENTATION..."

Here's another throwaway phrase, another waste of your query letter's real estate. Agent's know you're seeking representation. *They are literally reading your query letter.* Worse is when the author throws in an adverb: "I am humbly seeking representation" (as opposed to arrogantly?), "I am actively seeking representation" (as opposed to passively?), or "I am respectfully seeking representation" (as opposed to rudely?).

CHAPTER 6

THE FOUR-PART QUERY LETTER

PART TWO: THE PROJECT SUMMARY

THE PROJECT SUMMARY IS THE EASIEST PART OF THE query letter to write. It's one or two sentences that list your project's title, genre, and word count.

Title. Genre. Word count. Those are the nonnegotiables.

Other things to include are comparable titles (comps) and any accolades this particular manuscript may have received, if applicable. Comps and accolades sometimes appear with the title, genre, and word count at the top of the query letter. Sometimes they appear at the end of the query, as they can be a natural way to sum up your pitch. Either place is fine. Again, we'll look at some examples in a bit.

TITLE

Definitely give your book a title in your query letter, even if it's a title you're not 100% thrilled about. Your agent, editor, and publisher's marketing team will likely work with you to come up with a different title down the road anyway, something on-trend for its genre but also unique. Something that identifies your book as belonging on a certain shelf but also ensures it stands out and readers won't confuse it with some other similarly titled work. Coming up with the perfect title is hard, but querying your novel as "currently untitled" can work against you. A bad title is better than no title.

On that note, don't explain in your query letter that your title is temporary, that you don't like it, or that you're open to suggestions. No. Give your book a title and let it stand. Then move on with the rest of the project summary so you can knock 'em dead with your killer pitch!

GENRE AND WORD COUNT

Genre and word count tend to cause writers a lot of stress. Since different genres carry different word-count expectations, it makes sense to discuss them in the same conversation.

I said it already, but I'll say it again. Genre is not a dirty word. It's a useful way to help the industry most effectively get your book in front of the largest number of readers who are most likely to enjoy it. One of the best things you can do for yourself if you want to build a fiction-writing career is learn how to talk about what you write in terms industry folks use. Genre categorization speaks to readers' desires and expectations, and word count is a big part of that.

From aspiring or pre-published authors, I see a lot of manuscripts that are simply too long. These lengthy tomes are often written by authors who are convinced that every precious word, paragraph, and scene is critical to the work as a whole. In other words, either they've never received a professional edit, they've not yet learned how to self-edit (a skill that often comes after being professionally edited or through editing the works of others), or they've not yet mastered the rigorous disciplines of tight scene-craft, story structure, or pacing.

In any case, the word-count ranges typically considered reasonable within the traditional-publishing space are hardly difficult-to-hit targets. For acceptable ranges for particular *forms* of fiction, Science Fiction & Fantasy Writers of America (SFWA) offers the following under the eligibility requirements for its Nebula Award:

- Short story: less than 7,500
- Novelette: 7,500 to 17,500
- Novella: 17,500 to 40,000
- Novel: 40,000 and above

This is useful to a point, but be aware that 40,000 words is extremely short for a novel. It's appropriate for a middle-grade novel (novels written for readers in or around grades five through eight), but plenty of novels currently being published for that market are clocking in at 50,000 to 60,000 words. Even category romances—those slim little paperbacks you can pick up at the grocery store and read in a few hours—are 50,000 words or more.

In fact, at the time of this writing, the website of romance-publishing giant Harlequin lists submission guidelines for its twelve different lines. Five require that submitted manuscripts be a minimum of 50,000 words, four require a minimum of 55,000 words, and three require a minimum of 70,000 words.

So, yeah, 40,000 words is super short. Digital-only publishers may be less concerned with such things, but if your goal is to see your book published in print, you'll be hard pressed to find a Big Five publisher willing to make you an offer for a work that brief.

If we're talking about word-count ranges that are generally acceptable for *novels of particular genres*, here's what I'd offer:

- Literary/Mainstream/Women's Fiction: 80,000 to 110,000
- Crime Fiction/Thrillers/Suspense: 80,000 to 100,000

- Cozy Mysteries: 60,000 to 80,000
- Romance: 50,000 to 80,000
- Fantasy/Science Fiction: 90,000 to 120,000
- Paranormal Romance/Urban Fantasy: 70,000 to 90,000
- Horror: 80,000 to 100,000
- Historical: 90,000 to 120,000
- Young Adult: 70,000 to 90,000
- Middle Grade: 40,000 to 60,000

It's important to note that these ranges exist because readers of certain genres have certain expectations, and publishers—along with the savvy writers those publishers consistently buy manuscripts from—strive to satisfy those expectations. For instance, readers of category romances tend toward short, sweet stories they can consume in a couple hours, while readers of historical or single-title romance are game for a longer ride. Even then, there's only so long a writer can string out a will-they-won't-they romantic storyline before readers skip ahead to the good stuff. Or, worse, abandon a novel altogether. So in the romance space, on average, anything much longer than 80,000 words might, depending on the writer's skill at keeping their audience engaged, tax readers' patience.

Readers of cozy mysteries tend to enjoy a quick read. Cozies often feature quirky amateur sleuths as unlikely heroes and spare the reader the visceral, disturbing details and dark psychological trappings that readers of thrillers or other crime-fiction subgenres hunger for.

Readers of fantasy and historical fiction expect writers to build them an immersive story world, and readers of science fiction want to geek out on the science or technology, whether real or imagined, on which those stories are built. So in those genres, a longer word count is expected.

On the other hand, readers of paranormal romance (which delivers the plot beats and emotional impact of the romance genre) and urban fantasy (which delivers the plot beats and fast pace of the mystery genre) expect snappier reads, so higher word counts in those genres can be a tougher sell.

In general, know that if you are preparing to query your first novel, you are better off waiting until you can get your manuscript's word count within the appropriate range for its genre. Yes, there are exceptions—debut novels of 150,000 words or more that made it big, hit bestseller lists, got film or TV deals, and earned glowing accolades. Plenty of aspiring novelists can fire off at least half a dozen such exceptions in defense of their own lengthy word count. But please, please trust me when I say that, at the end of the day, if you're a debut author, you'll increase your odds of getting your foot in the door if you're the rule, not the exception.

Why is it so tough for an agent to sell in a debut novelist for a book of greater than 100,000 words? For one thing, longer novels require more time and resources to publish. When agents put hefty debuts out on submission, it's not uncommon for editors to cite word count as a reason they're declining to buy the book. Editors might say, "The book is really strong and the author is obviously talented, but I just don't have room right now to take on a manuscript of that length."

In addition, debut novelists are unknown quantities. Risks. Your agent and acquiring editor don't yet know what you're like to work with. Can you accept editorial feedback? Can you deliver stellar revisions? On time? Can you make *all* the deadlines spelled out in your contract? What are you like under pressure? Do you buckle down and get it done, or do you make excuses, flake out, or stop answering your agent's calls or your editor's emails? How do you react when you receive a scathing review or when a reader tears you down personally on social media? (Which *will* happen. Prepare yourself.) What about when a bookstore does a poor job of advertising your signing and no one shows up, or that convention where you've been invited to deliver a keynote speech forgot to order your books? Do you fly off the handle and lash out, or are you gracious under fire?

Your debut novel is your audition, and the process of

working with your team—your agent, editor, publishing house, and, eventually, booksellers, librarians, and event-organizers—to get it to the marketplace is like your probationary period as a professional writer. Once you've been through that process once and proven that you are, indeed, a team player who's ready for the pros, then it will be much easier for you to hit up your team with your proposals for more out-of-the-box ideas that will require higher word counts to execute.

Until then, your best bet is, again, to be the rule, not the exception. And that includes getting your manuscript's word count within reasonable, expected limits.

COMPARABLE TITLES

Comparable titles, or comps, are books or authors with established readerships that you're hoping to capture with your book. I can't stress enough how important it is that you include comps in your query, or, if you're sitting down with an agent or editor for a face-to-face pitch appointment, that you're prepared when they ask you (and they will) to name a comp or two.

Comps help you communicate in very few words where your book fits in the current market—pure gold when you're trying to grab and keep an agent's attention. I've read many a query pitch that's left me scratching my head because I can't pinpoint the intended tone. Does the author expect me to laugh or take this seriously? Is it morose or satirical? Then I get to the author's comps and it all makes sense. I understand in which market space the author envisions their work, and then I can re-read the pitch through the appropriate lens.

It's important to choose comps that are relatively new. The book market is constantly shifting, and within the market at large, each genre experiences its own shifts. Readers' tastes change. When you list an older comp—say, something published more than nine or ten years ago—the agent reading your query might assume that you aren't well read in your genre, that you're out of touch with what readers of your genre are currently spending their money on. Part of building and sustaining any career is keeping up with the times. The career of Professional Writer is no different.

However, it *is* OK to comp a classic, especially if you've written a retelling or mashup of sorts. Tales from, say, the ancient Greeks or Shakespeare are timeless, as are myths and folklore from all around the globe. Just be sure your query conveys what you did to make your retelling or mashup unique.

Also, be cautious about comping something that has more recently become part of your genre's cannon. For instance, when you say your book is like *Harry Potter*, *The Lord of the Rings*, or *A Game of Thrones*, it's hard for an agent to know what you're comping. That is, what exactly is in those books that readers will also find satisfying in yours? Such books and series are so sweeping, so epic in scope, that unless you get more specific about why you're comping them, it feels as though they're the only bestsellers or bestselling authors you can think of. Or, worse, it comes across as though you're claiming you're the next Rowling, Tolkien, or Martin, and while we all hope that's true, it's a premature claim that shoots right past confidence into industry-blind arrogance. Few things turn an agent off faster than declarations like, "I'm the next Stephen King/Nora Roberts/James Patterson. I'll make you $1,000,000, so it's your loss if you don't represent me."

In short, what you want to avoid is comping something more recently out of date, something that was on-trend a decade ago but wouldn't stand out in today's market. Don't chase the caboose of a train that long ago left the station.

The best way to ensure solid comps is to read. Read what's currently selling well, both in your genre and in others. I once attended a wonderful lecture by David Morrell, author of *First Blood* and creator of Rambo. He said that writers seeking to make a name for themselves in a particular genre should be able to stand up in front of an audience of their peers and deliver a lecture on the history of that genre. How did it begin? What are its roots? Which books and authors defined the genre, and which caused its greatest shifts? When did those shifts happen and why? Which writers influenced or informed other writers within that genre? Which books withstood the test of time to become part of the genre's cannon, and which, in contrast, didn't age well?

In essence, where has the genre been, where is it now, where might it be going, and how will you be part of the path forward?

None of this goes in your query letter, mind you. But I love what Morrell has to say here, and he's not the only successful writer who has said it: If you want to be a writer, *read.* Pay attention to what's going on around you in the fiction-publishing space. Many an aspiring novelist has told me over the years that they're too busy writing their own books to read other people's. Or when I ask them what their favorite books and authors are, or even what's the last book they read, they give me a deer-in-the-headlights stare. Few things raise my little red flag faster than that. Writers who don't read are laboring in a vacuum, making the writing life so much harder than it already is. Literature as a body of cultural experience is a conversation, and well-chosen comps demonstrate that you're part of it, and that you listen as well as speak.

Not only should your comps be current, they should also be relatively successful. List comps that have made bestseller lists, that have received critical praise, that have earned four- and five-star reader reviews, or that have been adapted for TV or movies. If you list comps that are on the obscure side, the chance that the agent or slush reader will recognize them is slimmer, and you'll have lost the opportunity to evoke that brilliant flash of understanding about your work.

Speaking of TV shows and movies, you can comp those too.

But wait! Didn't I just define comps as already-published *books and authors*? Yes, I did. But now I'm going to widen the field for you a bit. Books, besides belonging to the *literary* conversation, also belong to the much broader *pop-culture* conversation.

Comping non-novel media tends to work best in the speculative genres—science fiction, fantasy, horror, and their many subgenres—because, in the world of story, they are the richest pop-culture environments with the most active and loyal fandoms. Fans of TV shows and movies, as well as comic books, graphic novels, video games, role-playing games (RPGs), and cosplay do a lot of reading and book-buying. Well-chosen comps help identify which existing fandoms would be most likely to enjoy your book.

Comping TV shows and movies can work well in other genres, too. Romance writers tend to comp box-office-smashing rom coms, while mystery or thrillers comp moody, atmospheric movies or, if they envision writing a series, TV shows driven by a fascinating central character audiences return to again and again.

How do you talk about comps in your query?

The basic strategy is to provide a pair of comps. For instance, "will appeal to fans of Kristin Hannah and Celeste Ng" and "for readers who enjoyed Joe Hill's *Heart-Shaped Box* and Paul Tremblay's *A Head Full of Ghosts*" go a long way toward helping an agent see where you envision your book in the market.

But you can do better.

The cut-above strategy is to provide agents with an intersectional understanding of your work. The no-fail formula is "My book is X meets Y," where X and Y are particular *aspects* of your story that (a) your comped authors and titles are known for delivering and (b) readers love. These aspects include but aren't limited to:

- Tone, mood, or atmosphere
- Type of protagonist, cast of characters, or relationship between characters
- Trope or plot device
- Voice or prose style
- Story structure
- Pace or amount of action
- Theme

With this formula, you have the opportunity to make your comps work so much harder for you. Now, instead of "will appeal to fans of Kristin Hannah and Celeste Ng," you can say "is an unlikely-friendship story in the vein of Kristin Hannah's *Firefly Lane* set in a suburban dystopia like Shaker Heights in Celeste Ng's *Little Fires Everywhere*." Other examples:

> It offers readers the fast pace and immersive world of *Black Panther* with the slow enemies-to-lovers burn of Sally Thorne's *The Hating Game*.

> The multiple-timeline, multiple-POV structure of N.K. Jemisin's *The Broken Earth* trilogy meets the psychological paranoia of *The Girl on the Train* by Paula Hawkins.

> The thrill-a-minute action of Blake Crouch's *Dark Matter* meets a quirky and lovable *Ocean's Eleven*-style cast of antiheroes.

> The lyrical, upmarket prose of Erin Morgenstern's *The Starless Sea* with the snarky, badass heroine of Tamsyn Muir's *Gideon the Ninth*.

In the end, good comps do two things. They help you get your query read through the correct, most focused lens, and they communicate which pre-existing—and hopefully large—audience is most likely to enjoy your book. Choose your comps wisely!

ACCOLADES

If the manuscript you're querying has earned any accolades, mention that as part of your project summary. Like comps, accolades can appear either at the top of your query or just after the pitch. Did your manuscript win or make the finals in a writing contest? Mention it! Did a well-known author or editor read your manuscript in whole or part and give you some positive feedback? Mention that, too, though only if the author or editor is well-known enough that the agent reading your query would recognize the name.

My caution here is that you keep your accolades brief. Your query letter is not the place to write out in-depth quotes or blurbs verbatim, like you see on the covers of published books. A quick mention of an accolade can get an agent's attention, but it won't sell your manuscript. Only your pitch can do that.

PROJECT SUMMARY PITFALLS

Since title, genre, and word count are the nonnegotiable components of the project summary, and comps are super-duper highly recommended, we already know the first pitfall is leaving one or more of those things out. But what are some other pitfalls to avoid in the project summary?

CONVOLUTED TITLES

I read dozens of queries every week for books called things like *The Gods of Malforesia: Part One: Deliverance* or *Battleground: The Wars of the Kings and Queens of Malforesia, Book the First*. These are often, but not always, by fantasy writers who are trying for a title that (a) evokes a sense of epicness and (b) communicates that this is the first book in a series.

Don't confuse your series title with the title of the first book. And don't forget that you are only pitching book one. You have to sell book one before you can sell book two, and so on. So if you have a colon, comma, or "book one" (or similar) in your title, you have an opportunity to do better. Your best bet when giving your book a title is to give it *one* title. *Just one title.* You can worry about naming your series and numbering the installments later.

PAGE COUNT INSTEAD OF WORD COUNT

One of the quickest ways to communicate that you're brand-new to the industry is to give your manuscript's page count instead of its word count.

Before I went to work in publishing, I taught junior-high language arts. That was a long time ago, back in the days when teachers who assigned any kind of writing project had to reserve time in the computer lab weeks in advance and troop the entire class down the hall for a word-processing session. This was before smartphones and tablets and laptops. (OK, there *were* laptops back then, but they weighed more than a toddler and cost thousands of dollars, so only corporate executives carried them, usually in leather shoulder bags the size of microwave ovens.) This was even before it was reasonable to expect that students or their parents had a computer in the home.

All this is to say, I've seen lots of creative ways that very few words, whether handwritten or typed, can be stretched to meet a five-page minimum requirement.

Page count is moot.

Even in pro publishing, book designers can manipulate a manuscript of a certain word count to fill just about as few or as many pages as they want. Font size, margins, and leading (rhymes with heading; the vertical white space between lines of text) can all be tweaked to influence the overall page count. So your letter should reference your manuscript's word count, not it's page count.

Not the word count *and* the page count. Just the word count.

Not the page count plus a rundown of which font, font size, margin size, spacing, etc., you used. Just the word count.

And not the word count down to the exact number of words. If your manuscript clocks in at 87,521 words, just query it at 87,000 or 88,000 words. There are no points to be lost (and no red flags to be raised) by rounding up or down to the nearest thousand.

CROSSING TOO MANY GENRES

We've already talked quite a bit about genre and its role in helping industry pros identify a book's audience—step one in getting it in front of as many readers as possible. Here, we're going to expand on that conversation a bit.

Cross-genre works exist. These are novels that deliver the familiar tropes of more than one genre, often in a fresh, unique way. You might hear this and think, "Brilliant! If I write something that's both a police procedural and an epic fantasy, then readers of both genres will buy my book!" Or, "My book is science fiction but it's also Raymond Chandler-esque noir, so it will appeal to both audiences!"

You might be right. I hope you are. There are certainly plenty of fantastic books out there that fit not only these particular descriptions, but any number of Genre-X-meets-Genre-Y mashups.

But I do have a couple cautions for you.

First, if you write cross-genre works, make sure your expectations are realistic. In fact, you're better off not mentioning market- or sales-related expectations in your query letter at all. The truth is, many cross-genre books divide a potential audience rather than double it. Avid readers of the speculative genres (sci-fi, fantasy, horror, and their many subgenres) tend to be far more open to reading works cross-pollinated with other established genres (mystery, romance, historical, etc.), but readers who "don't read any of that dragons and wizards or spaceships and laser-guns stuff" tend to be genre purists. Even if you promise them a tight mystery plot and sparse prose reminiscent of Raymond Chandler, these readers are far more likely to bail the first time your main character curls his bionic fingers around the stock of his photon whip.

In fiction, speculative elements are like curry: add even a pinch to your dish, and it can't be anything else but a curry dish. Something to keep in mind if you're crossing a speculative genre with a non-speculative one.

My second caution is to avoid making up your own genre. I think some readers do this to sound smart. Others are trying to try to stand out—to communicate that their work defies the reductive and pedestrian system of genre classification. Still others simply don't know what they're writing or who it's for; they know only that they have written something, and they'd like someone to help them get it published. Whatever the case, weird, made-up genres will most likely begin to raise an agent's little red flag. What is a "metaphysical dystopian memoir," how many readers are looking for such a thing, and where would an agent begin to look for an editor to acquire it?

My final caution is to avoid crossing too many genres. "This science fiction police procedural is an epic family drama with strong romantic elements set in a dystopian world based on 1930s Chicago" is so splintered that many agents and editors might not even know what to do with it or where to begin. But could a story like this work? Absolutely. It's all in the execution and the skill of the writer. So how do you query it? Describe it as simply as possible here in the project summary, and then spend your energy crafting a pitch that transports us into the worlds, lives, and plights of your characters. Let the pitch do its job.

"FICTIONAL NOVEL"

A novel is, by definition, fiction. So when I see "fictional novel" or "this novel is a work of fiction" in a query letter, I already have the sense that the author isn't quite ready for the job of Professional Writer.

INCOMPLETE MANUSCRIPT

I mentioned this before, but I'll say it again: It's important that your manuscript is complete before you begin querying. If an agent likes your query enough to request your manuscript, then they want to read it *now*, especially if market timing is on their mind (and market timing is always on an agent's mind). Many a writer has disclosed in their query letter that their manuscript isn't done yet, and that alone will most likely make for a quick pass.

Every once in a blue moon, I get one of these "my book's not done yet" queries, but I'm really intrigued by the pitch. In that case, I might dash off a quick, personalized note inviting the writer to resubmit when the novel is complete. But this kind of thing is super rare and not something you should expect.

HOW LONG THIS NOVEL TOOK YOU TO WRITE

The length of time it took you to write your novel is not the selling point you might think it is. If your first novel took you ten years to write, then how long will it take you to write your next novel? An agent is thinking, "If I sign this writer on as a client, how long will it take them to finish something new that I can sell?"

Keep in mind that if an agent signs you, and then sells your debut novel to a Big Five house in a two- or three-book deal, you will most likely be given one year to write each subsequent book under that contract. One year per book. If you've heard authors on panels at writing conferences tell aspiring novelists in the audience to enjoy how much time they have to write their first novel, this is why.

On the other hand, if you say in your query that you wrote your book in ten days, an agent might not even glance at your pitch. Ten days, or even a couple of months, is not enough time to write a novel that's likely to stand out, let alone be competitive, in the Big Five space.

Agents are very familiar with NaNoWriMo (National Novel Writing Month, which happens every November), during which more than 100,000 authors from all around the globe work to write 50,000 words in thirty days. NaNoWriMo is awesome! The accountability, sense of community, and encouragement to quash the inner critic and just write are valuable experiences for writers who often toil away in isolation and self-doubt.

However, if you participate in NaNoWriMo in November, your novel is not ready to query in December. Or January. Or February, March, or even April. A draft that started out as a quick exercise in writing hot will take time and multiple drafts to revise—to shape into a satisfying, well-paced, and well-crafted story.

Querying your first draft is not a solid strategy, nor is admitting in your query letter that you know your manuscript is rough but you're open to revisions. If you know your novel isn't ready to query, don't query. And you had better be open to revisions! You're applying for the job of Professional Writer, and all Professional Writers need editors, so your openness to being edited must go without saying.

"THIS IS THE FIRST IN A TWELVE-BOOK SERIES."

When I first started working at Nelson Literary Agency, my primary job was to audit our clients' royalty statements. (For more on how to read a royalty statement and to learn how publishing accounting works, see my book *Do You Need a Literary Agent?*) For each client, I would produce charts showing how each of their titles was performing over time, tracking unit sales, earnings, returns, and more. Using this information, our clients could make data-driven decisions about their careers.

One thing these charts showed over and over again is that series tend to fizzle after about book four or five. Fewer and fewer readers buy each new book in a series, until publishing new books in that series no longer remains cost effective for the publisher. Industry folks know this. No one's handing out contracts to debut authors for more than three books at a time. And if you're a debut who landed a three-book contract, you're a rare and lucky bird.

There are, of course, exceptions—long-running series that readers still can't get enough of. But those series caught fire later, after two or three books were on shelves awhile and publishers had time to recognize that they were sitting on a potential gold mine. The point is, the authors of such exceptional series didn't pitch a six-, eight-, twelve-, or twenty-book series.

They pitched one book. The first book. Because if the first book doesn't sell, then the rest of the series won't sell either.

The function of your query letter is to sell one book.

Is it OK to mention that you're working on a sequel? Or that you envision this book as the first in a trilogy? Of course! But I'd recommend you stop there. Anything more could indicate that you're not familiar enough with how the industry works or that you have unrealistic expectations.

A standard phrase many writers use in their query letters—and you can, too!—is "this is a standalone with series potential." Agents want to net you a multi-book contract. Every contract negotiation they do takes hours and hours of their time over weeks or even months, so two or more books for the time-and-effort price of one is good business. If you envision your novel as a standalone, but you can truthfully say that you are willing and able to write a sequel, then use this standard phrase in your query letter. Otherwise, indicate that it's a standalone and leave it at that.

"MY FRIENDS AND FAMILY LOVE THIS BOOK!"

My response to this is that your friends and family love *you* and they want you to be happy. Though they may also objectively love your book, mentioning in your query letter how much your friends, family, children, grandchildren, etc., love your book doesn't come across as the professional endorsement you're hoping for. If you're compelled to cite endorsements in your query letter (and trust me when I say your query letter *does not* need endorsements), then you're better off with legit praise, if you have it, from established authors, editors, or other industry folks the agent you're querying is likely to know of.

But again, you do not need endorsements in your query letter. Your query letter is all about the strength of your pitch, and a strong pitch won't need much, if any, propping up.

MARKET RESEARCH OR MARKETING PLANS

In your query letter, avoid telling your prospective agent about the publishing market. A good agent knows more about the publishing market than you do. Period. In fact, that's probably why you're trying to get one to represent you. I hope.

When you say things in your query like, "Very little

fiction has been published for people who..." or "No novel has ever been published about a character who..." or "Today's readers are ripe for...," you're running the risk of sounding ill-informed and poorly read. An agent or editor might be able to rattle off ten recently published novels about whatever it is you think "no novel has ever been published about," so you're better off spending your energy pitching your novel rather than identifying whatever hole in the market you think it fills. Identifying a void in the market is a best practice for nonfiction books, but it's not necessary in the fiction space.

Furthermore, your query letter is not the place to talk about your plans for marketing your book. Telling an agent you're available to go on an international book tour is cart-before-the-horse stuff. Again, step one in this whole process is to get an agent interested in reading your full manuscript. That's it. That's the sole function of your query letter. After that, there's a gazillion other things that need to happen before it's appropriate to talk about book tours or other marketing efforts.

What about social media? Should you mention which platforms you're active on and how many friends and followers you have on each? In chatting with agents at conferences I've attended over the years, I believe it depends. For some agents, it's important that debut authors are already active on social media, maybe even have a website or blog. Other agents don't give a rip where a debut author can currently be found online. As long as your book is killer and they know they can sell it, you're in. But do know that once you're in, you will be expected to build at least some online presence and maintain at least some level of social-media activity.

If you don't know whether you should mention your social-media presence in a query letter to a particular agent, be sure to read that agent's guidelines carefully. Maybe they mention wanting to know. If the agent uses QueryManager, they can choose to include fields on their submission form that require you to fill in your website or Twitter handle, so assume if those fields are present, they want to know. Otherwise, you're safe leaving all that out.

CRITICIZING ESTABLISHED BOOKS OR AUTHORS

One of the fastest ways to earn a rejection from me is to criticize established books or authors. Tell me how stupid you thought *The Hunger Games* was, tell me how insipid you find Stephenie Meyer's writing, tell me how authors today just aren't writing intelligent or worthwhile fiction, tell me how you decided to become a writer because you read *Fifty Shades of Grey* and knew you could do better, and I'm out.

This sort of thing tells me far more about you than

it tells me about your ability to write. Even if your pitch is awesome and your sample is solid, an agent who had to wade through arrogant barbs to get there probably doesn't want to work with you. If you work hard, you're willing to keep learning, and you're a team player, there's room at the top for you. You don't need to claw your way up the backs of other writers to get there.

EXAMPLES OF GREETINGS AND PROJECT SUMMARIES

We've just looked at the first two parts of a query letter (the greeting, which is optional, and the project summary, which is not) and several pitfalls to avoid in each part. You can easily roll these two parts into one succinct paragraph—keeping in mind that, as discussed, it's OK to move comps and accolades to the bottom of the pitch, as they do feel like a natural way to sum up the pitch and transition to the bio.

Here are some examples I've pulled from actual queries we've received, altered only to protect writers' identities. Some are better than others, but most would keep me reading. I've included a bit of commentary on each to help you craft your own query's opening.

> I saw in your bio on the Nelson Agency website that you represent single-title romance novels. I'd like to take the opportunity to share with you

> my romantic suspense novel, *Title*, complete at 90,000 words and set in Northwest Washington D.C.

OK, I did mention earlier that quoting an agent's website in your first line isn't the strongest, most standout way to open your query simply because so many writers do it, but I also mentioned it's not grounds for an auto-reject. All told, this is still a solid intro. It includes a title, genre, and word count. The phrase "I'd like to take the opportunity to share" could simply be "I'd like to share." Wordiness in your query makes me worry about wordiness in your manuscript, so look for places to tighten.

> After you looked at my first finished novel, *Title A*, last summer, you requested that I query you with my next project, after it was completed. My second young adult novel, *Title B*, is now complete at 75,000 words, and I wanted to send it to you first.

Pretty good! The writer mentioned that the agent read prior work and invited them to submit again. Definitely something to mention right away. The phrase "after it was completed" is extraneous and can be cut (the author mentions that it's complete in the sentence that follows), and young-adult is a market or category, not a genre. (Is it young-adult *fantasy*? Young-adult *historical*?

Contemporary young adult?) But all told, we have a personal connection, title, and word count, so this is an intro that would keep me reading.

> I read your Agent Spotlight in *Writer's Digest* and saw that you are actively seeking young adult fiction. I think you may like my realistic young adult novel, *Title*. Currently at 77,000+ words, this novel is set in Charlotte, NC and explores homelessness and poverty.

Solid enough. I'd read the pitch. But the word "actively" can go, the word "realistic" should be "contemporary," and the phrase "currently at 77,000+ words" makes me worry the novel isn't complete. Avoid ambiguity! Also, although we have a personal connection, plus title, genre, and word count, we also have a setting and a couple of themes. Setting and theme aren't part of your project summary and should be worked more elegantly into the pitch itself.

> NLA has always been my top choice for representation due to your professionalism, advocacy for authors, and participation in community conversation. Two years ago when I queried Angie Hodapp at Fancy Conference, she requested a partial. While it was not a good match in the end, I was encouraged to keep going thanks to her kind words. I now have a new manuscript…

This writer does of great job of establishing a personal connection. (Plus it mentions me! Yay!) It transitions nicely to the project summary, which starts with "I now have a new manuscript…" But I include this intro here because it's hovering at the max amount of real estate you want to devote to such things. We like knowing we are your top agency, but let's get to that pitch!

> I am querying you because you are looking for STEM girls and voice driven contemporary. I believe you will be interested in my YA Contemporary, *Title*, complete at 81,000 words.

Nice. It's all there, though there a couple minor mechanical errors present. But I'm definitely continuing on to read the pitch.

> I'm currently seeking representation for my YA-adult crossover novel, *Title* (61,000 words). Given your interest in science fiction and thrillers, I thought it would be a good fit for your list.

Again, "I'm currently seeking representation" is a generic opening. Not grounds for an auto-reject, just… generic. Shoot for something more specific to the agent or agency. Something more unique. My red flag is starting to climb the pole with the descriptor "YA-adult crossover." Every author hopes their novel will appear to more than one market, but there are no publishers out there expressly looking for YA-adult crossover novels. An agent will have to decide whether to shop your manuscript to YA imprints or to adult imprints. Maybe they'll shop it to both, but if your manuscript truly straddles the line between these two readerships, then an editor at a YA house will ask you to age it down, and an editor at an adult house will ask you to age it up. Both would require a major rewrite of your manuscript. So as a slush reader, I'm already concerned that this writer doesn't understand the market or what crossover means.

In addition, 61,000 words is light for YA, and it's *really* light for adult…especially given the query's next line, which mentions science fiction and thriller, two genres in which higher word counts are typical because readers expect an immersive read. And is it a sci-fi thriller? Or just sci-fi? Don't muddy the waters. Nail that genre! If this query opens with so many red flags, would I really read the pitch? Sure. I'd at least glance at it. The intro is so brief that the pitch is *right there* in the next sentence. I read so fast that my eyes wouldn't be able to stop themselves. But with so many red flags already raised, one more and I'd be out.

> I hope this finds you well. We met at Lighthouse Writers Workshop's LitFest last June. I enjoyed our conversation and wanted to reach out since I'm now ready to query agents! I am seeking representation for my work of literary fiction

> with commercial appeal, *Title*. The completed manuscript is 92,000 words in length and reminiscent of Laura McBride's *We Are Called to Rise* and Ruth Ozeki's *A Tale for the Time Being*.

Here's a good example of an intro that includes comps. Again, your comps can appear with the rest of the project summary, like this, or they can appear at the end of your pitch. I'd cut "I hope this finds you well," which sounds like the opening line of late-nineteenth-century correspondence, and that exclamation point sticks out like a sore thumb. As Kristin Nelson's slush reader, I recognize the phrase "literary fiction with commercial appeal" because she lists it on our website as something she's looking to represent, so that works. Overall, given the diction here, I'm not surprised that this is a literary writer. There are some opportunities to tighten the query, but I'd definitely move on to the pitch.

> My debut novel, *Title* (99,000 words), is a work of literary fiction that explores the consequences of family secrets kept and revealed. It was a finalist in the 2018 San Francisco Writers Conference Contest.

Nice! Succinct, with a title, genre, and word count right up front, plus it gives an accolade. That definitely made me sit up and pay attention. As you already know, I'm not a big fan of leading with themes, but the author didn't linger, and it *is* literary fiction, which places a greater emphasis on theme than most genres. And anyway, this is another opening that's so succinct that I'd already be reading the pitch before I had a chance to decide not to.

> After learning of your work with one of my favorite authors, and your preference for voice and character driven stories, I believe we are a perfect match to work together. I would love to have the opportunity to be represented by you with regard to my book, *Title*. As someone who recently started a second career in a very competitive field, I recognize the advantages of working with someone with the drive to succeed in a difficult career.

This one's a tad problematic for me. First, why not mention which author? As a slush reader, I'm already suspicious that this is a generic query poorly disguised as a personalized one. "Perfect match" and "love" are gushy and borderline unprofessional. And overall, this intro is wordy. The phrases "to work together," "to have the opportunity," and "with regard to my book" should be cut and the title worked in more elegantly elsewhere. The bit about starting a second career in a competitive field, etc., is irrelevant to your query. Leave it out. Get to the pitch! The further down your query you make an agent's eyes travel before they land on your pitch, the more likely they are to lose patience.

> While reviewing your website, I noticed you are seeking voice-driven women's fiction. I believe my novel, *Title*, might be a good fit for you. At 115,000 words, *Title* is a complete women's fiction novel set in the intertwining worlds of present and past New Orleans from multiple points of view. Here is a bit about the story.

By now, you recognize the ubiquity of that opening phrase, so enough said. This intro isn't bad, but it trips over itself a couple times: both the genre and the title are mentioned twice (once is enough). In addition, the word count is high for the genre, and the setting should be more elegantly worked into the pitch, which we haven't gotten to yet. Finally, "here is a bit about the story" is a clunky and unnecessary transition. So does this opening make me worried about this writer's ability to communicate clearly? Unfortunately, yes.

My hope is that looking at these examples was helpful to you and that your own query letter's greeting and project summary are beginning to take shape. In any case, it's time now to move on to the big show: the pitch!

CHAPTER 7

THE FOUR-PART QUERY LETTER

PART THREE: THE PITCH

OK. This is it. The main event. The part of your query letter that should take up the most space on the page. The part that carries the most weight in an agent's decision whether or not to request your manuscript.

No pressure.

Seriously—no pressure. Take a deep breath. We're going to walk through it together.

But before we do, know that while I'm going to include a few snippets of examples here and there—examples I've written myself for illustration purposes—this book does not include complete samples of query letters. That's because you can Google "query letter examples" and come up with plenty to see online for free. I'd recommend you start with queryshark.blogspot.com, where you can read more than 300 query letters submitted to Query Shark since 2007, each deconstructed and critiqued in great, no-holds-barred but constructive detail. Perusing that blog is definitely worth the investment of a few hours of every aspiring writer's life.

Regardless, I definitely recommend what I call the bookstore exercise.

THE BOOKSTORE EXERCISE

Here's the first thing I advise writers to do when they're new to querying: Clear your schedule for an afternoon and head to your favorite bookstore. Bring a notebook and pen; you'll find out why in the next section. Order your favorite beverage. Then camp out on the floor in your genre's section and read the back-cover copy (or flap copy, if you're looking at hardcovers) of fifty novels.

Back-cover copy is sell copy. Whether it's written by the book's author, agent, editor, or someone in the publisher's marketing department (most likely, it was written by some combination thereof), its purpose is to entice readers to buy the book. Your query's pitch is sell copy, too, written to make an agent think, "I can sell this!" Your reading the sell copy for fifty novels in your genre is like a musician warming up by playing scales. It will loosen you up and tune your ear to the voice of professionally written sell copy—from the rhythm and phrasing of the writing itself to the way the characters, world, conflicts, and stakes are presented, and how anticipation for the story is built over the course of only a few brief sentences or paragraphs.

Can't you just go to Amazon and read the descriptions for fifty novels online? No. Go to the bookstore. Support the industry you're applying to work in, even if you're just buying a cup of coffee. But also, the problem with some online descriptions is that they aren't constrained to the space available on the back or inside flap of a book, so they might not be as concise as your query's pitch will need to be. Also, you're more likely to find newer titles published by Big Five publishers on bookstore shelves. Newer titles are more relevant to your genre's current market, and pro-published books represent the type of artifact you're hoping your book will become with an agent's help in the traditional-publishing space. You will walk away from this exercise with two things: a much better sense of how to write sell copy, and a wide overview of fifty books that made the traditional-publishing cut.

Ideally, as you're pulling books off the shelf, you'll pick some you've previously read all the way through. That way, you'll see that not all characters and subplots get mentioned in the sell copy. The same will be true of your pitch. And, of course, you'll pick some books you haven't read yet. This will allow you to think critically about whether the sell copy has done its job. Are you as a reader excited by this pitch? Not excited? Ambivalent? Why? How much of your relative interest in reading the book is due to its similarity to something you've already read? How much to its being so completely different from anything you've ever read before? How much because you've heard positive buzz about the book—friends have recommended it, it has earned a spot on a bestseller list, or it has received lots of positive reviews? Did the buzz affect your reading of the sell copy?

The bookstore exercise will also reinforce for you how personal book-buying choices really are. Our experience of story is subjective. Likewise, agents and slush readers are bringing their personal tastes to each day's slush pile. There's no such thing as an objectively good book that everyone will love. When you internalize that, your skin may get a little thicker, which is a good thing, and you may find it easier to keep your torch lit during the query process.

THE FIVE W'S

OK, here's why I asked you to bring a notebook and pen to the bookstore with you. For each book you pull off the shelf, write five W's down the left edge of a page in your notebook. These stand for:

- Who is the protagonist?
- What do they want? (Goal)

- Why do they want it? (Motivation)
- Why can't they have it? (Conflict)
- What happens if they don't get it? (Stakes)

As you read the back of each book, see if you can identify and write down the answers. In well-written sell copy, you should be able to find most if not all of the answers to the Five W's.

WHEN, BUT, NOW, MUST, OR (ELSE), BEFORE

As you're working on this exercise, look for sentences or clauses that start with "when." "When" is not one of the five W's, but it often shows up fairly early in a pitch, because but it signals a disaster or a significant interruption in the protagonist's ordinary life. This might be the novel's inciting incident, first plot point, or some other conflict that is significant to the plot as a whole. Examples:

> When Sarah's husband is killed in a car accident…

> When Ben accidentally delivers Jake's note to the wrong girl…

> When one of the alien ships lands in Mark's backyard…

> When Elizabeth finds an antique key in her grandmother's jewelry box…

> When Rohan is stripped of the crown that is rightfully his…

Also look for sentences or clauses that start with "but," which often signals conflicts, complications, obstacles, or other bumps in the road for the protagonist:

> But Sarah's husband was keeping a devastating secret: he stole $700,000 from the Russian mob.

> But Ben can't bring himself to tell Jenny that Jake wrote the note for Tracy, not her.

> But no one believes Mark, not even when he shows them the burnt patch of grass where the ship touched down.

> But the key doesn't fit a single lock in Elizabeth's grandmother's house.

> But Rohan's sister is raising an army—if she cannot keep the throne by rights, she will keep it by force.

Next, look for sentences or clauses that start with "now," which signals the protagonist's new and very bad situation, or their plan for how to overcome whatever was introduced by the "when" and "but" statements. In addition, you'll probably see a "must" or two pop up around this point in the pitch. "Must" signals that the protagonist has no choice. Circumstances have forced them into a corner, into making an impossible decision, or into a situation they cannot turn their back on:

> Now on the run, Sarah must figure out what her husband knew and where he hid the money—or the next brakes the Russians tamper with will be hers.

> Now, rather than humiliate Jenny by telling her the truth, Ben decides to convince Jake to fall in love with Jenny instead of Tracy. The problem is, Ben might be falling for Jenny himself.

> Now, Mark must figure out how the alien device works and what, exactly, it does before his husband has him committed to the state mental hospital.

> Now, Elizabeth has only one chance to fit the key into the correct treasure box and only one guess whether to turn it left or right, or a Pandora's Box of evil will be unleashed upon the world.

> Now, Rohan must turn to the only person who can help him defeat his power-hungry sister: his sworn enemy, the great sorceress Naliah.

Notice that "now" and "must" statements might also include "or (else)" or "before." These are your opportunities to build stakes into your pitch. In the sentence "now X *or (else)* Y," X should be something very, very, very difficult if not downright impossible for your protagonist to do, whether physically, mentally, emotionally, or spiritually. Y should represent either literal death for your protagonist or a fate worse than death. Maybe Y is that the whole world is in jeopardy if X doesn't happen. Maybe a whole city or village will be destroyed. Or a family. A child. A job. Money. Status. Love. Whatever your protagonist stands to lose, make it bad for them. Make it so bad for them that we as readers know in our bones that your hero would rather die than face such a devastating loss.

Likewise, in the sentence "now X must happen *before* Y happens," *before* gives us a timeline, a sense of urgency, a ticking clock—always a great way to shift a story into overdrive. Again, make sure X is something nearly impossible for your protagonist to face or accomplish (whether internally or externally), and make sure Y is death or worse (whether literal or figurative). We'll look at stakes more closely in a bit.

PREPARING TO WRITE THE PITCH

If you completed the bookstore exercise (and if you did, I commend you!), you're almost ready to start writing your own pitch. Maybe you have a completed manuscript. Or maybe, like we talked about in Chapter 1, you're writing a pitch for an idea you have, and you want to test it out, make sure you have all the makings of a complete, compelling, salable story. Whatever the case, turn to a fresh page in your notebook and—you guessed it—write the five W's down the left.

For your own story, write down the answers to each W. This isn't your sell copy yet, so don't worry about making it pretty. You're just putting the answers down on paper so that (a) you can reassure yourself that they are present in your manuscript, and (b) they are front and center in your mind as you prepare to write your own pitch or sell copy.

My guess is, if you completed the bookstore exercise, you're already starting to hear the pitch for your novel taking shape in your head. Compelling phrases and sentences are starting to spring up on the page. This is good! Go with it.

Once you've answered the five W's for your manuscript, it's possible one of two things has happened. You might have written something that's too long so you'll need to cut it down, or you might have just a phrase or two for each that you'll need to beef up. Or maybe, just maybe, you clocked in at the perfect length, something that after a little polishing will fit on one page. Whatever the case, let's look next at honing each element of the pitch.

HONING THE CHARACTER PART OF YOUR PITCH

If you're on the heavy side, remember that not every character and subplot in your manuscript need to appear in your pitch. If you're stymied about whom to include (this often happens to writers who've written multi-POV stories, which for this very reason are notoriously difficult to pitch), then look at which character's POV came first in your manuscript. There's a reason, subconscious or otherwise, that you started your story with that character, and whether or not you intended for this to be the case, the first character a reader meets in a novel is often the character they identify as the main protagonist. Order signals primacy. Regardless, the character(s) whose arcs you include in your pitch should satisfy a few criteria:

- Is that character's arc the most compelling?
- Does that character's story carry the highest, most profound, or most far-reaching stakes?
- Do that character's decisions and actions have the greatest impact on the other characters in the story, compared to how much impact other characters' decisions and actions have on the rest of the cast?
- Which character's arc presents the most interesting hook? In other words, which character's arc is most likely to make an agent, editor, or reader sit forward in their seat and say, "I have to read about this person to find out what happens to them!"

When you evaluate each character in a multi-POV or ensemble-cast story based on these criteria, your stars quickly stand out from your supporting cast. Your pitch should focus on your stars and their arcs.

If, on the other hand, your compiled answers to the five W's fall on the light side, then you have an opportunity to add to your pitch. What are you leaving out that could ultimately serve to get an agent interested in reading your full manuscript?

Let's start with the first W: Who is the protagonist? Perhaps you have an opportunity here to give us a touch more insight into this character. You don't want your pitch to dwell on the protagonist's backstory. After all, it's *this* story that you're trying to sell, not any stories that happened before page one. But did your protagonist endure some backstory event—some trauma in their past, *before page one* of your manuscript—that will inform how they think, react, behave, emote, and, most importantly, *change* over the course of your novel?

This backstory event is often referred to by story doctors and developmental editors as the wound event, and it has a very specific function in a story's overall structure. In short, it kicks off the protagonist's *internal* conflict, which, in well-structured stories, is resolved along with their *external* conflict, which is introduced by the inciting incident *after page one* of your manuscript.

Here's a fun fact: Writers who include prologues are often, without realizing it or being able to articulate why their gut told them their novel needed a prologue, doing so because they want to get the wound event on the page. And you know what? For that purpose, prologues are A-OK.

Does your character have a wound event? Is that something you can include or hint at in your pitch while resisting the urge to dive too deep into a lengthy explanation?

Another way to beef up your first W is to give us a few words about your protagonist's ordinary world. Who are they before they get walloped by your novel's inciting incident? And your inciting incident should pack a wallop; otherwise, it probably lacks the necessary fuel to propel your protagonist and their story into the upper stratosphere of intrigue and excitement that readers of commercial fiction demand.

If you're familiar with classic story structure or the three-act model, you'll recognize "ordinary world" as the first step in the hero's journey. Ordinary world is the establishing shot that hints at how the protagonist will change by the story's end. Reluctant now? Willing later! Follower now? Leader later! Meek to bold. Alone to connected. Cold and closed off to emotionally vulnerable and caring. Selfish to generous. Ignorant to knowledgeable. Spiritually lost to enlightened. Addicted to sober. Unable to able. No-fun rule follower to super-fun adventurer. Or any of these in reverse. The number of character arcs writers can choose from is limited only by the vast landscape of human experience. Identify your protagonist's arc, and then perhaps hint at their ordinary world in your pitch—again, resisting the urge to dive too deep into a lengthy explanation. A few words should suffice.

Beware of omitting character from your query letter altogether. Believe it or not, we do see query letters fairly regularly that don't mention a protagonist at all. Instead, they focus on the story's world or premise. I'm looking at you, speculative-fiction and historical-fiction writers! Whether you've built a made-up world from scratch, complete with its own geography, climates, seasons, resources, flora, fauna, history, class structure, spiritual beliefs, etc., or you've done extensive research about a particular time and place in history, you've forgotten to tell us who, specifically, is going to have an adventure in your story's world. I respect that world building and historical research are lots of work. But be careful that world is not all you're pitching in your query letter.

In character-omitting queries, there are often *people* (groups of humans, human-like beings, aliens, gods), there is often conflict (a Big War looms between races, factions, societies), and there are often stakes (the fate of the world, the future of X-kind). But with no hero mentioned in the query, there is no promise of an internal journey, an emotional plight. There is little to ground the reader in such an epic world, little for readers to latch onto.

Remember that character is plot and plot is character. You can't have one without the other.

HONING THE GOAL PART OF YOUR PITCH

The second W, *what does your protagonist want?*, should also be something with enough spice to whet readers' appetites. I read no small number of query letters each week that pitch the internal conflict: "Protagonist wants to find out who they really are" or "Protagonist wants to discover what they're really made of." Writers assume that because they have "want" on the page, they've established goal. But they're wrong.

I can't encourage you strongly enough to scratch the internal conflict from your pitch. Or, if you need to include it, do so subsequent to the external conflict. In commercial fiction, the protagonist's goal must be external. They have to go places, do stuff, move around in their physical space, and be acted upon by their environments and by other people or forces within those environments. Can they have internal goals, too? Of course! They must! But we're talking about your pitch here, and unless you're writing literary fiction, internal stuff isn't particularly pitch worthy.

Think of your pitch like a movie trailer: How excited would you be to see a movie (art-house cinema aside) where the trailer shows a character sitting alone in a room with a brooding look on their face because they're ostensibly struggling with their inner demons? Yawn. In a well-structured commercial novel, the internal change occurs *as a result of* the external action. As a slush reader, I can't picture the external story I'm in for with the pitch, "Luke wants to grow up, accept more responsibility, make friends, have adventures, and discover what great things he's capable of," but I sure as heck can picture, "Luke wants to jump in an X-wing and blow up the Death Star to save the galaxy from an evil empire."

When it comes to nailing the protagonist's goal in your pitch, beef it up by cutting way back on the internal conflict. Devote that real estate instead to your story's movie-trailer moments.

Some query pitches are built around a weak story goal. Something we see quite often is "Protagonist just wants to be normal." That's fine. It's a perfectly legitimate, realistic, and relatable goal for a person to have. And it certainly sets us up neatly for a reluctant-hero story, such as Protagonist discovers they have special powers they never asked for and don't want, or Protagonist develops a condition that sets them apart from their peers, or Protagonist endures a life event they couldn't control and now everything is different.

If this is the type of story you've written, recognize that "Protagonist just wants to be normal" is an ordinary-world, character-establishing statement, *not a statement of your story goal.* In your pitch, we're looking for the goal that will drive your plot. What happens once your protagonist is forced to accept that "normal" just ain't gonna happen? What becomes their goal after they begin to exercise their agency? Is it to use their newly developed powers to rescue their little sister from kidnappers? Ah! There's a goal that's clearly stated and strong enough to drive a compelling plot, so that's the type of goal I want to see in your pitch.

Another thing you might be struggling with as you craft the goal part of your pitch is *which* of your protagonist's goals to pitch. In plenty of novels, and perhaps in yours, the protagonist has multiple goals. For example, a typical YA pitch these days (typical because it's fine but not particularly fresh or unique) presents a protagonist who *wants* to get good grades because they *want* to get into their dream college because they *want* to become a doctor (or whatever). That's three goals!

Except not really.

This is a string of goals: the protagonist has to achieve A before B and B before C, with C—becoming a doctor—being the ultimate goal. But ask yourself: Is "Protagonist wants to become a doctor" the goal the drives the plot of your novel? My guess is no. My guess, after reading tens of thousands of query pitches for contemporary YA, is that these particular wants/goals are part of the protagonist's ordinary world. When you read that string of goals, can't you just feel the rumble of the inciting incident rolling toward you down the plot tracks? Sure, protagonist wants the grades, the college, the career…*but then something happens to threaten all that.* And in the wake of that something, the ordinary world crumbles, and the plot-driving goal emerges…

Maybe the inciting incident is that one or both parents dies or loses their job, and paying for tuition at Fancy University just isn't going to happen. Now the actual story goal (not the ordinary-world goal) is that the protagonist must come up with the money to pay for college. This means the conflict and stakes (which we'll talk more about later) that you throw down in front of your protagonist will be relevant to money: Protagonist has to compete for a scholarship, but it's only a partial scholarship. Protagonist doesn't qualify for full financial aid. Protagonist has to take a low-paying, undesirable job. You get the picture.

Or maybe there's a new kid at school who is just as smart as Protagonist, maybe smarter, and they're both after the same goal—say, the title of valedictorian or the lone internship position that will sparkle on a college application. Now the actual story goal is that the protagonist must beat New Kid to the accolade, and the conflicts and stakes you throw down will be related to that: Protagonist develops romantic feelings for New Kid, complicating the competition between them. Protagonist is the youngest of seven children, and all six of her older siblings were named valedictorian of their graduating classes, so the pressure's on. Protagonist cheats on a final exam in their desperation to be the best and either gets caught, or doesn't and must decide whether to confess and concede that New Kid won fair and square. Again, you get the idea.

Be sure you know the difference between ordinary-world goals and plot-driving goals. It's OK to put the ordinary-world goal in your pitch, but don't devote a lot of real estate to it. State it succinctly, and then move on to state and develop as necessary the goal that drives your plot.

Here's the quick formula: "All Protagonist ever wanted was X, but when inciting incident happens, everything changes. Now Protagonist must Y." Do you see some of those pitch buzzwords we talked about in a previous section?

Here's an example of a pitch that wastes valuable real estate by over explaining the protagonist's ordinary-world goals:

> It's the start of senior year, and all Sarah wants is to ace her classes—AP bio, AP chem, AP everything—so she can get a full-ride scholarship to Harvard's pre-med program. Then it's on to med school, after which she's sure to land a residency at the Mayo Clinic. And after that, she'll become an orthopedic surgeon and specialize in sports rehabilitation, a field she became interested in when her older brother, Seth, broke his leg playing football. Sarah is determined to be not only the first doctor in her family, but the first person in her family to go to college. Maybe she should be worried, but she knows she's got this in the bag. Every year since kindergarten, she's been at the top of her class. Only one year to go, and she can move on to achieving her dreams. But first, in order to get the full-ride scholarship she needs, she has to land that internship at the local hospital, and every year, they only accept one high-school senior…

Look at how much space is wasted on setup and backstory! By the time an agent has read that many lines of text in a query letter, they should know a great deal about the story already. Are you as a reader beyond ready to find out what the actual story is going to be? I am. when I read pitches that start out this way, my eyes, if they don't glaze over, skip down the page, looking for a juicy story problem I can sink my teeth into.

Let's revise this pitch, paring down the ordinary-world goals and devoting more space to the plot-driving goal:

> High-school senior Sarah Smith has her sights set on Harvard Med and a career as an orthopedic surgeon. But then Jason Jones, the new kid in town, applies for the one internship Sarah knows will land her a full-ride scholarship. And for Sarah, no scholarship means no college. The worst part? Jason is smart. Really smart. But Sarah needs that internship…even if, for the first time in her life, she has to lie and cheat to get it.

This is pretty close to a complete pitch, but a verbal one. It's too brief for a query pitch. In a query letter, use the space available to you to really flesh out the pitch and sell the agent on requesting your manuscript. With that in mind, this pitch would go on from here, developing additional conflicts (maybe romantic feelings, getting caught cheating, etc.) and raising stakes. The point is, this rewrite manages in far less space to establish not only the ordinary-world goal (in the first sentence), but also the plot-driving goal (to land the internship no matter the costs). It also gives us an inciting incident (Jason applies for the internship Sarah needs), a couple complications (Jason is legit competition, Sarah is willing to compromise her values), and even some stakes (no internship, no scholarship, and no scholarship, no college).

This is the type of word economy to strive for as you're crafting your pitch. If you find yourself going down any particular rabbit hole, explaining more than needs to be explained, then back yourself out and start over.

Here's yet another type of story that might trip you up as you're honing the goal part of your pitch: the story in which the protagonist's goal changes. Maybe as the protagonist learns new information, meets new people, or begins to change and grow over the course of the plot, what they wanted at the beginning of the story doesn't wind up being the goal they achieve (or don't) at the end. Let's look at how to address this problem—which might not turn out to be a problem at all.

We now know that (a) a protagonist can have both ordinary-world goals and plot-driving goals, (b) these are not the same thing, and (c) they are often separated by an inciting incident. But there's a third type of goal: *scene* goal. Scene goals are a series of micro goals that a protagonist must achieve on their path from page one to the end of a novel. In other words, the protagonist will duck, dodge, weave, feint, confront, trip, fall back, regroup, analyze, etc. (whether physically, intellectually, emotionally, or spiritually), on their quest for the information, skills, and resources they need to achieve the story goal. Each maneuver is most likely presented in a distinct scene, and each scene requires your protagonist to set a micro goal and either achieve it, not achieve it, change it, or abandon it. Whatever the outcome, it affects what your character decides to do next, and to what degree that decision will have been emotional or logical. Essentially, your protagonist breaks down their big story goal into lots of little scene goals that you, the author, string together as you move your protagonist toward your novel's resolution.

When you're writing your pitch, avoid confusing your story goal with your scene goals. I've seen many a pitch get lost in the weeds because the author wanted to convey one particular scene they are certain is so compelling and unique that it alone—and not the pitch for the overall story—will entice the agent to request their full manuscript. It might work, but most likely, it won't. Agents are looking for the 30,000-foot view of your novel so that *they* understand that *you* understand story structure, and that you're pitching a complete work that will keep a reader turning pages for several hours.

Plenty of story goals come prepackaged inside their genres. In crime fiction, the story goal is to catch the villain. In courtroom dramas, to convict or acquit the defendant. In supernatural horror, to defeat a non-human or invisible entity. In romance, to overcome resistance and surrender to love. In women's fiction, to navigate a shift in life circumstances related to family, friendships, career, or some combination thereof.

Your challenge, besides knowing what *general* goal readers of your genre want to see attained, is to figure out what goal is *specific* to your protagonist. What do they want *in addition to* your genre's general goal? Why is the novel *this* protagonist's story as opposed to any other detective, attorney, ghost hunter, ingénue, or woman dealing with a life challenge?

If you're having a hard time answering that, my concern is that there's a problem with your manuscript. You might have written either an everyman protagonist—a generic hero the reader can slip into like a suit, who exists on the page only to go through the motions of your plot—or a lens character, who exists only to observe the often more interesting actions of other characters in the novel but exercises little agency or drive of their own.

If, on the other hand, you can immediately differentiate your genre's general goal from your protagonist's specific goal, then you can use that to hone your query. Work both goals into your pitch: the first to reinforce that this is, indeed, a story that belongs in the genre you identified in your project summary, and the second to establish that you've written an interesting character with a unique goal that has great potential to hook readers.

If you're still struggling to articulate your protagonist's specific goal, then you might have written a more episodic novel—say, a novel in which your character hops from situation to situation, encountering a series of conflicts that are altogether unrelated, or perhaps loosely related by secondary characters, theme, setting, etc., resolving each before moving on to the next. We see this a lot in stories that feature quests, puzzles, or trials. The deadly phrase in a query letter that gives away an episodic novel is *along the way*. We'll look at examples of *along the way* queries later, in the section called "the wandering protagonist."

Episodic novels are not necessarily bad. They can work. But from what we see in the slush pile, they often signal that the author, though perhaps accomplished at writing gorgeous prose and compelling scenes, has not yet mastered the novel as a form. In a novel, there's a dramatic throughline that can be traced from the first page to the last. An author drawn to writing episodic works may be better suited to shorter forms, such as short stories or novellas. Or they may be compelled to explore literary fiction, which is granted much greater latitude when it comes to structure and letting internal conflict as opposed to external steer the barge.

However, I've heard many an aspiring novelist attempt to pitch their novel into the commercial space while also referring to it as literary. Usually, this is an attempt to pre-emptively excuse a lack of structure or a shortage of the expected conventions of a particular genre. In general, avoid using the word literary to describe your genre novel. I'd advise you to use it only if you know for certain—because you are so well read—that you have, indeed, written a crossover novel. Can you carry on a face-to-face conversation with an agent about the differences between commercial and literary fiction, and how your novel fits both descriptions? Or are you calling your novel crossover because you aren't really sure how to talk about this book you wrote or where it would fit in the current market?

In sum, when addressing goal in your pitch, it's OK to touch on your protagonist's ordinary-world goal and your genre's general goal. Avoid leaning too hard against your favorite scene's micro-goal, no matter how compelling, poignant, or revelatory that scene may be. Know what your protagonist's main story goal is—often hidden in the "will she or won't she" story question—and work from there.

HONING THE MOTIVATION PART OF YOUR PITCH

Motivation—why does your protagonist want their goal?—is sometimes implied within the goal itself. Hero Mark Watney in Andy Weir's *The Martian* wants to survive on Mars long enough to be rescued. His goal is to not die. Do we as humans really need to understand the *why*, or motivation, of that goal? No. We get it because we'd want the same thing if we were in his shoes.

However, drilling down to your protagonist's true motivation can be a valuable exercise in story development. Have a conversation with yourself that feels like having a conversation with a toddler—your inner story toddler, if you will. Maybe the conversation goes a little something like this:

"My character's goal is to find the 400-year-old treasure chest rumored to be buried on Shipwreck Island."

"Why?"

"Because he's a treasure hunter. He's the *best* treasure hunter. He's found every relic he ever set out to find except for this one treasure chest. It's the one thing that has eluded him." (Ooh! Opportunity to develop this character's obsessive nature or blind faith or both, plus some backstory and how he's viewed by others in the treasure-hunting community as well as by the locals in the places he goes to hunt for treasures.)

"Why?"

"Because it's really hard to find, and lots of other treasure hunters have looked for it and failed to find it, and maybe it doesn't even exist." (Ooh! Opportunity to introduce cool secondary characters and plot conflicts with other treasure hunters.)

"Then why look?"

"Because...because he has something to prove." (Ooh! To whom? Opportunity to develop a backstory character and Protagonist's wound event.)

"Why?"

"Um...because...OK...because his father was also a treasure hunter, even better than Protagonist is, and they used to hunt for treasures together, and his father died looking for this particular treasure chest, and Protagonist couldn't save him, and all the antiquities experts who say it doesn't exist think Protagonist's father was crazy."

Ooh! He wants to find the elusive treasure chest (goal) because he wants to redeem his father's reputation. Now there's a compelling motivation we can build a story around, with lots of opportunities for both external and internal conflicts.

Obviously, much of this sort of deep drilling should be done before you write the book or as you revise it. Regardless, by entertaining our inner story toddler, we've arrived not only at some great opportunities for story development, but also at a compelling motivation for our pitch. Let's take a look at our pitch before we drill down into true motivation:

> All Protagonist wants is to find the 400-year-old treasure chest rumored to be buried on Shipwreck Island because he's a really good

> treasure hunter and this is the only relic that has eluded him.

This is…fine. But as we know, fine is the enemy of great. As far as motivation goes, it doesn't really connect Protagonist to his goal on an emotional, gut-punch level. Instead, let's try this:

> All Protagonist wants is to find the 400-year-old treasure chest rumored to be buried on Shipwreck Island because his father, the greatest treasure hunter of his time, lost his sanity, his professional reputation, and ultimately his life looking for a relic archeologists have long called a myth. Only by finding the chest can Protagonist prove his dad wasn't crazy and redeem their family name in the eyes of the academic world.

Why stop there? We could go even further with our inner story toddler: Why is redemption in the eyes of the academic world so important to Protagonist? Maybe that's a question Protagonist has to answer for himself through the course of the novel as he risks his own life looking for the chest. Maybe one of these antiquities experts can become a sidekick or even a love interest for Protagonist, grounding him in reality or making him question his quest. ("Just accept that the chest is a myth and move on! Get back to work finding things that can actually further the world's understanding of whatever ancient culture.")

Maybe we can even add a twist: What if, when Protagonist finds the chest and opens it, he discovers something that links his own ancestors to the pirates who stole it, or to the monarchs they stole it from? Any opportunity you find to tie the protagonist more tightly to the core of the story, take it!

Are you starting to see how this works? Motivation plays a major part in that idea I mentioned earlier, that character is plot. When you drill down into what people want and why they want it, and then explore the actions they are willing to take in pursuit and what they're willing to risk—plus throw in a few juicy, fat obstacles and an antagonist or two—you have the ingredients of story. The deeper you go, the more times your inner story toddler asks why, the deeper the character becomes, and the more opportunities you have to add dimension to your novel.

So how can you put this to work when writing your pitch? Well, your manuscript may already have all that depth-of-character built in (I hope it does!), but the mistake you want to avoid in your pitch is stopping after you answer the first "why." If you do, your pitch might be… *fine*. But it's likely an agent won't feel compelled enough to request your full, and all that development you did in your manuscript may go unread and unappreciated.

If you're having a tough time identifying your protagonist's motivation, then I'm going to warn you:

You're going to have a tough time selling it into the commercial space. Literary? Maybe. But commercial? It'll be a long shot.

Here's an example—a typical one that I see all the time in our query slush—of a story pitch with no motivation:

> When Protagonist finds a box of letters in her grandmother's attic, all signed *Yours, E.* and dated between 1942 and 1945, Protagonist decides she must find out who wrote them.

OK. Sure. Finding a box of letters like that would be cool. It would make a lot of people curious, so it's a plausible and relatable goal for a protagonist to have. However—and this is important—*curiosity alone isn't a strong enough motivation to drive the plot of a commercial novel.*

This writer has to go deeper. All writers who feature a protagonist driven by curiosity over some historical or family mystery need to. *Why* does Protagonist decide she must find out who wrote the letters? What bearing does the solving the mystery have on her life or current situation? How will it radically change things for her in the now? Does she suspect her grandfather isn't her own mother's biological father? OK…*why* does that matter to her? Is there a genetic condition at play? An inheritance? You're a storyteller: What circumstance can you weave into Protagonist's motivation here that would add a sense of conflict and urgency to your story?

When you can answer that, *that's* what you should pitch.

Plug in the variables: "Protagonist must find out X before Y or else Z." If Y is some sort of ticking clock, and Z is something really bad that Protagonist must prevent, then you're on your way to being able to articulate your protagonist's motivation. But if you're stuck after "Protagonist must find out X," you might need to revisit your manuscript and go back to the story-craft drawing board.

Finally, motivation, like goal, should be so personal and inextricably tied to character that it can't be shared by any other character in the novel—at least not in the exact same way. For instance, let's say you're writing a YA mystery in which three teens set out to solve the murder of a small child who lived in their neighborhood. It's not enough for the pitch to say, "Henry, Kylie, and Joel must solve the murder before the killer kills again." Sure, that's a good start, but it only addresses the mystery genre's generic motivation—that is, the motivation that every protagonist in every murder mystery shares: to prevent the killer from killing again.

What you must do in your pitch (and before that, your manuscript) is go deeper and give us your three heroes' individual motivations. That's what's really going to make your book stand out from others like it. Henry needs to find out who the killer is because his cousin is a suspect and he wants to prove his cousin's innocence. Kylie needs to find out who the killer is because she thinks her little sister, the victim's best friend, was the killer's actual target. Joel needs to find out who the killer is because he's in love with Kylie and wants to help her solve the mystery…or so you would have readers think. Plot twist! Joel has known all along who the killer is, and he's only involving himself in his friends' investigation to derail them and keep them from getting too close to the truth.

You wouldn't pitch that big reveal, of course—you'd tease us with it. You'd pitch each character's motivation, and then conclude with something evocative, like, "But the closer they get to finding the killer, the closer they get to a terrible truth: one of them has known all along who the killer really is."

The point is, in doing just this much, you'll see myriad opportunities to develop each character and build varying degrees of reader sympathy for each. These are characters who will keep secrets from each other, who will occasionally act alone, who will leverage each other for personal gain, and so on. By exploring *character* at this level, you will begin to develop *story*.

HONING THE CONFLICT PART OF YOUR PITCH

The fourth W asks why your protagonist can't achieve their goal or get what they want without a fight. The fight part is conflict. What kind of conflict often depends on your genre.

Let's review the classic dramatic conflicts you most likely learned in high school English.

Person-versus-Person (PvP) conflicts are exactly what you'd expect: two people pitted against each other, whether because they are after the same goal that only one of them may attain; because they are after opposite and mutually exclusive goals; or because they have a vested interest in the other person's failure (if A gets their goal, something really bad will happen to B).

PvP is the most classic type of conflict, and it's the most common in commercial fiction because it gives us the greatest opportunities to create visually exciting and relatable clashes on the page. It can fuel main plotlines as well as subplots. It can work in any genre.

In mysteries, thrillers, superhero stories, and some horror (any hero versus villain situation), PvP conflict is resolved with a final and very physical battle that comes down to who can outsmart and outmaneuver whom. After a few dead bodies along the way, climax and resolution involve handcuffs, weapons, daring escapes or rescues, courtroom justice, etc.

Other types of stories that rely on a physical PvP conflict are sports stories, like *A League of Their Own*, which pits two sisters against each other on the baseball diamond, one more talented, the other more passionate. This is also a touching sister story, so there's the added value of an emotional PvP conflict and a teary reconciliation as well.

In romance, PvP conflict is emotional in nature, resolved only when the characters in conflict accept that love conquers all. PvP conflict also takes on an emotional cast in family dramas and women's fiction, wherein characters confront each other over long-held secrets, old resentments, fresh wounds, or misunderstandings, and may or may not reconcile.

Person-versus-Nature (PvNature) conflict is also just as it sounds. These are survival stories, like *Castaway*, that require the protagonist to survive against seemingly insurmountable odds in a harsh environment (a deserted island, Mars, Antarctica, a disabled submersible at the bottom of the ocean), with nothing but their own their cunning and ability to innovate with limited resources. PvNature also includes stories about large-scale threats to humanity: volcanic eruptions, earthquakes, meteors, tsunamis, and pandemics, to name a few. Add in other survivors to any of these scenarios, and you can play with both PvP and PvNature conflicts in the same story, as many survival and doomsday stories do. I'd also put forth that any person versus wild animal, cryptid, or other beastie falls into this category. However, once you give a non-human opponent the ability to reason or strategize beyond its own survival instinct, you've elevated the ways in which the conflict can be escalated and resolved, so I'd categorize that type of conflict as PvP conflict.

PvNature conflicts have an inverse: PvMachine. In the former, nature is the antagonist. In the latter, the protagonist represents nature as a positive force standing against the folly of that which man has created. The antagonist can be anything from literal robots, cyborgs, or superhuman artificial intelligence to manmade disasters: oil spills, reactor meltdowns, or nuclear winter. Cli-fi (climate fiction, post-apocalyptic stories about the fallout of various types of human-caused, and therefore tragically preventable, environmental collapse) would, by this definition, fall under the PvMachine umbrella.

Person-versus-Self (PvSelf) conflict gives us a story more focused on the protagonist's internal journey than on their external one. For that reason, you're most likely to find stories rooted in PvSelf conflict in literary fiction than in commercial fiction. Does that mean commercial fiction can't feature characters who battle internal demons? Who are struggling to figure out who they are and what they're made of? Who are concerned with what it means to be a good person and live a good life? No.

Absolutely not. Characters in *all* types of fiction should experience at least some degree of internal conflict. If they don't, they're cardboard cutouts, two dimensional and inherently uninteresting. But just because your story features a character with an internal conflict doesn't mean you're telling a PvSelf story. So as you're preparing to craft your pitch, make sure you're clear on the difference.

Person-versus-Group (PvGroup) conflicts pit a protagonist against a group of people, whether small (a family or group of colleagues) or large (a neighborhood, school, village, city, kingdom, cult, political organization, corporation, church/religion, etc.). This is also where you'll find characters standing against systemic forces that are invisible, like racism, sexism, homophobia, and so on. The key here is that the group or institution is greater than the sum of its parts, making it all the more difficult for the protagonist to defeat or sway. And even if the protagonist has an ally inside the group, the ally is too entrenched in the group's norms to be of any substantial aid. In PvGroup conflict, the group in question is institutional, so it comes preloaded with a prescribed set of rules, norms, beliefs, regulations, and, most importantly, consequences for those who step beyond its bounds or outright oppose its supremacy. PvGroup conflict is either resolved when the protagonist topples the group (as in *Mockingjay* by Suzanne Collins); takes control of the group and becomes its new leader (as in the 2008 movie *Doomsday*, one of my guilty pleasures); or assimilates, whether by choice or by force (as in *One Flew Over the Cuckoo's Nest* by Ken Kesey).

Finally, **Person-versus-God (PvGod)** conflicts give us stories about crises of faith, morals, ethics, beliefs, and spirituality. These stories don't have to feature the god of any particular faith as a character, though they may; if they do, they are often seen or heard by the protagonist only. PvGod is the cousin of PvSelf stories in that both lean heavily on the protagonist's internal conflict and journey. PvGod stories often involve soul-searching, prayer, meditation, peace-seeking, and guidance from a wise elder or mentor character, as well as moral dilemmas or tests of spiritual fortitude.

Note that PvGod conflict also drives a lot of spiritual or religion-based horror. Stories about exorcism, for instance, often include a Catholic priest as a character, and it's not unusual that he's suffering some internal crisis of faith even as he's invoking Christ in an attempt to free someone of the demon possessing them. Any horror story that relies on the audience's belief in a particular religion for its jump scares, or in angels, priests, prayer, crucifixes, holy water, or other religious rituals for the story problem's solution have some element of PvGod conflict.

By the way, many writers today play with classic world

mythologies and superhero tropes, and plenty of these writers even create secondary worlds, and then create religions for those worlds and make the gods of those religions actual characters on the page. Don't be fooled: These stories are not the stuff of PvGod conflict. Rather, they are examples of PvP conflict because the gods are humans with special powers. Their desires are petty, their weaknesses their downfall.

Overall, these classic conflict types are useful to review—especially now, as you prepare to write your pitch. It's important that you know which conflict type forms the foundation of your novel.

What you shouldn't do, however, is be too on-the-nose within the pitch itself. Statements like "this novel features a classic Person-versus-Nature conflict with some overtones of Person-versus-Person and even a chapter in the middle that's Person-versus-Self" are obvious and inelegant. Your novel's conflict type should be clear within the pitch itself. For instance, if your pitch is fundamentally about two grown sisters squaring off over the best way to care for their aging mother, then I know its main conflict type is Person-vs-Person. If your pitch is about a kid who's the lone survivor of a plane crash in the Canadian Rockies, you've set me up to expect a Person-versus-Nature story.

It's likely your novel features more than one type of

conflict, and that's OK. But which takes center stage? Not sure how to answer that? OK, let me frame it a different way: If Hollywood were to adapt your novel for the big screen, which of the classic types of conflicts are they going to feature most prominently in your movie trailer?

Let's look at an example. The movie *Jurassic Park* features plenty of PvP conflict because our cast of characters—scientists, mathematicians, biologists, tech wizards, visionaries, even children—all disagree about whether this park that crazy capitalist John Hammond created was a good idea. At first, their conflicts are theoretical, rooted in professional, emotional, and ethical debate. Later, however, after the dinosaurs get out, the story shifts to PvNature. Each major character winds up in a situation where they are alone against one or more dinosaurs. Because the dinosaurs are not humanlike—they are beasts acting on their completely natural instinct to hunt and eliminate threats—we know that's PvNature.

So is this a PvP story, a PvNature story, or both?

Hands down, *Jurassic Park* is PvNature. No one who hears the words *Jurassic Park* thinks first about the ethical disagreements among the scientists. They think about the dinosaurs. They think about that epic roar the T. rex lets loose when its massive jaws emerge from the darkness and the rain high overhead. They think about the clever velociraptors hunting in packs.

Therefore, if you were to write the pitch for *Jurassic Park*, the PvNature conflict is what you would focus on developing. No need to devote much real estate in your pitch, if any, to all the theoretical PvP disagreements among the cast in the story's first act. There are other PvP clashes toward the end of the movie as well—people whose actions become obstacles to our heroes as they try to get off the island alive—but they are just that: obstacles. Complications. They exist to raise the stakes for our heroes, but the main conflict is still those dang dinosaurs.

Classical dramatic conflicts aside, the next place to look as you're honing the conflict part of your pitch is in the specifics of your story. Let's start by revisiting your manuscript's dramatic throughline or overall arc. First, ask yourself this simple question: "Does my protagonist succeed or fail at the end?" Then ask: "What did they succeed or fail at doing?"

The answer to that second question should be the goal you developed for your protagonist from page one. If you're like a lot of authors, your story changed as you wrote it. The characters took on lives of their own, wanting things you didn't know they wanted, knowing things you didn't know they knew, taking actions you didn't expect. Maybe one of your core cast died along the way, and not even you saw it coming!

As a result, what I often see when I'm reading slush manuscripts is that the second half isn't what I as a reader was set up for in the first half. Many manuscripts take a left turn somewhere in the second act. Most agents or editors will hit that turn and stop reading. Or, if it's a manuscript written by an existing client, they'll point to the shift and say, "Rewrite from here to the end."

However, sometimes the better solution is to point to the shift and say, "Keep everything from here to the end and rewrite the beginning."

I've noticed that some second halves are better than first halves. That's because by the second half, authors have spent more time with their characters, or they've allowed themselves to explore story events or twists that didn't occur to them back when they were plotting. Or maybe it just took them a while to hit their stride. In any case, a big mistake any writer makes is reaching the end of their manuscript and not re-evaluating whether the beginning still fits.

If you're having a tough time crafting your novel's pitch because you can't easily articulate its throughline or plot arc, your manuscript probably needs work.

If that's ringing a bell, then your story's two halves might not fit together the way they need to. Start by deciding which half (let's say chunk—it doesn't have to be exactly half) of the manuscript you like better or think is more compelling. If it's the first chunk, then make sure the second chunk knocks down the pins you set up. If it's the second chunk, then go back and rewrite the first, setting up the proper pins. Whatever the case, writing your pitch will be much easier once you get the throughline straight and on the page. And that's when you'll be ready to query.

Why am I asking you to look at goal and throughline when we are supposed to be talking about conflict? Because the goal or story question that launches your throughline *prescribes the specific conflicts* that you, the author, throw down in front of your protagonist.

Remember our example of the YA protagonist who wants to go to Harvard Med and become an orthopedic surgeon? If the story question is, "Will Protagonist earn the money she needs for college?" then the major conflicts you set before her will be economic in nature. We'll see her struggle with getting a job. We'll see her struggle when she realizes how undesirable that job is. She'll struggle to land an awesome internship only to find out it's unpaid. She'll apply and be turned down for scholarships, and so on.

If the story question is something different, like, "Will Protagonist beat New Guy for the coveted internship without falling in love with him?" then the major conflicts you set before her will be romantic and emotional in nature. We'll see her struggling to resist New Guy's charms. Listening to her divorcing parents tell her that education and career are the only things that matter. Dealing with her best friend who has developed a major crush on New Guy, and so on.

Knowing that your manuscript's throughline informs your plot's major conflicts is the first step in identifying those conflicts. Then you can make sure those are the conflicts around which you are building your pitch.

In commercial fiction, a protagonist is going to come up against all manner of hardships and setbacks from scene to scene. They need cash, but someone on the bus stole their ATM card. They need to get to San Francisco tonight, but the last plane left five minutes ago. They want to go to the party where they will accidentally-on-purpose run into the girl they have a crush on, but they came down with a cold. In general, these are scene conflicts, micro conflicts, bumps in the road. Differentiate them from the big-picture conflicts you crafted to keep your protagonist from too easily attaining that throughline goal.

HONING THE STAKES PART OF YOUR PITCH

This is it. The final W. What happens if your character doesn't get what they want? What happens if they don't attain their goal? In other words, *so what?*

The answer to *so what* is stakes.

That might sound harsh, but if you can't answer *so what* about your own story, then you can't reasonably expect readers to. The *so what* is what makes readers care. It's what gets them invested in an outcome that they're willing to spend several hours of their life turning your book's pages to discover. It's what makes them willing to spend $25 or $30 on the hardcover edition of your next novel.

It's also what many aspiring novelists neglect to include, both in their manuscripts and in their pitches.

Low stakes can be just as deadly as no stakes. "There's nothing at stake" and "the stakes were too low" are common reasons agents give for rejecting a manuscript, or for bailing on a manuscript before they read to the end. And it's incredibly difficult, if not impossible, to go back and add stakes to an existing manuscript without doing a pretty major rewrite. That's because the relative intensity of what's at stake for a character at any given moment will affect the decisions they make on the page. That's going to change the plot. Significantly. So if you've heard from an agent, editor, critique partner, or beta reader that your story needs higher stakes, buckle up and get to work.

A few years ago, I got invited to poker night at a friend's house. I decided I better learn to play. I looked for poker apps I could play against, but I was quickly frustrated because every single app required me to enter a credit card number and play with real money. Lame!

That's when I realized: poker *is* stakes. Stakes are inextricable from every decision you make in poker, and, furthermore, you make different decisions when the stakes are low than you do when they're high. Anyone who claims to have learned poker without having to ante up didn't actually learn poker. All they learned were the rules and mechanics of the game.

The same is true of story. A story without stakes is just rules and mechanics. It's ink on a page absent emotion, adrenaline, the prickle of sweat beading on the forehead, a sharp intake of breath, or the weight of knowing so much rides on whatever you decide to do next. Stakes are your character's skin in the game.

In a lot of commercial fiction, the stakes are life and death. Your protagonist is fighting all the way through your story to stay alive. Maybe they need to evade a killer, whether human (typical of crime fiction) or otherwise (typical of horror or supernatural thriller). Maybe they need to survive a massive battle or assassination attempt (typical of science fiction or fantasy). Maybe they need to stay alive in an extreme environment (typical of science fiction or fiction about natural disasters or castaway scenarios). Maybe they need to overcome a life-threatening injury or diagnosis (typical of mainstream, book club, or women's fiction). The list goes on. Your protagonist may also be fighting to keep a loved one safe from these types of deaths, or they may be a martyr, ready to sacrifice their own life on moral grounds or to save an entire people from certain death or devastation.

In literal life-and-death stories, both the motivation and the stakes are inherent in the pitch, so it's easy to confuse the two. Remember when we talked about Andy Weir's *The Martian* in the section on honing the motivation part of your pitch? Let's review: What does protagonist Mark Watney want (goal)? To stay alive alone on Mars long enough to be rescued. Why does he want it (motivation)? Because he doesn't want to die. What happens if he doesn't attain his goal (stakes)? He dies.

That sounds redundant, but it's still useful to answer each of the five W's for your story, just so they're clear in your own head and you can keep them straight as you prepare to write your pitch. But yes, the truth is, as soon as you pitch a character who's trying to stay alive, we can pretty much deduce both motivation and stakes.

What about stories in which literal death is not at stake?

Totally fine! However, to make sure your story is still built on stakes high enough to support a commercial novel, articulate how what *is* at stake is either like death or worse than death. The word we're looking for here is *loss.*

Does your protagonist stand to lose the love or trust

of another character, whether lover, parent, child, sibling, or friend? If so, then your novel needs scenes that paint a clear, vivid picture of the relationship between your protagonist and that other character. We need to see what beauty and value that love or trust adds to your protagonist's life so that we experience dread when you threaten to take that relationship away.

Does your protagonist stand to lose some measure of security? If they don't achieve their goal, will they lose their home? A large sum of money? Food during a famine or water during a drought? Will they lose their title or standing in polite society? Some opportunity to get ahead in life? Their reputation among their peers? If so, then your novel needs scenes that establish what your protagonist's world looks like *with* those things so that we experience dread on their behalf when we imagine them *without*. Your novel might even need what we call a stakes character, someone appearing relatively early in the novel who has already lost the thing the protagonist will later be in danger of losing. Stakes characters are effective because they give both the protagonist and the reader a clear glimpse of the worse-than-death outcome that loss represents.

In your pitch, state clearly what your protagonist stands to lose. What they are risking, whether knowingly or not? Is it life, love, trust, security, resources, social standing, reputation, something else, or some combination? Have a friend read your pitch, and then ask them to tell you what's at stake. If they can't do it, you might need to hone a little more.

The idea of rising stakes simply builds on this concept, upping the ante for your protagonist as the story progresses. For instance, early in the novel, your protagonist might do something in pursuit of a goal that puts him at risk of losing a large sum of money. The loss will devastate him (show us how much he needs that money!), but he wants his goal so much that he's willing to risk it. Then a chapter or two later, either he loses the money or he doesn't. If he loses it but still hasn't achieved his goal, then he has to push boundaries, risking something bigger (someone else's money, his car, his home, a kidney, his wife's kidney) because he's still in pursuit of his goal. If he doesn't lose the money, then he achieves a small victory. But because the story isn't over yet, the goal posts move. Something happens that forces him to risk something greater than money. And so on in cycles until he has nothing left to lose and arrives at the story's climax for a reckoning.

Let's look at an example so you can avoid the low-stakes/no-stakes mistake.

Say you're pitching a YA about Sam, who wants to make the basketball team (goal) because he wants to impress Janie, a girl in his biology class (motivation), but Sam is short and uncoordinated (conflict), plus the team has a new coach this year, a real macho dude who doesn't care much for Sam because Sam dinged his sports car in the grocery-store parking lot over the summer (more conflict), and Janie just started dating Brad, the varsity team's star point guard (even more conflict).

Do we have a story here? Not yet. We have a few key ingredients of story, but we're still missing the most crucial one: stakes. *So what* if Sam doesn't make the basketball team?

Based on this pitch, we can assume Sam will be disappointed. But—and this is important—*disappointment is not stakes.* Not in the commercial-fiction space, where stakes have to be high enough to drive the plot. So how do we recast our idea?

One answer is to make it not merely disappointment but *crushing* disappointment. Soul crushing. So soul crushing that it will damage Sam's identity and sense of self, affecting him negatively for years to come, if not for the rest of his life. How do you do that? One way is to layer in multiple sources of looming disappointment that will crush not only Sam's soul, but the reader's as well. Let's give it a try.

If Sam doesn't make the basketball team, he will not only (a) be disappointed, but also (b) not get the girl, (c) cause his older brother, Mike, whom he adores, to lose the $500 bet Mike made with their father over whether Sam would make the team, and (d) cause his father, whom it turns out was best buds with Coach Manly-Man back when they were in high school (another opportunity for conflict for Sam), to win the $500 bet with Mike and forever earn the right to keep calling Sam a pansy. If Sam makes the team, his father has to retire the insult for good. Now, there's much more than mere disappointment at stake for Sam if he doesn't make the team. There's a piece of his identity at stake that, if lost, can never be regained.

Can you imagine your older brother and father making a $500 bet over whether you'll make the basketball team, and your father betting against you? Furthermore, can you imagine your own dad calling you a pansy? Wouldn't you as a reader cheer a lot louder for Sam now than you would have if we'd stopped our story-development process with our original no-stakes idea? The very real possibility that Sam won't make the team makes readers feel like they're on a runaway train speeding downhill toward emotional disaster. Indeed, emotional death. That's stakes.

If you can turn disappointment-based stakes into stakes that threaten to damage a character's identity or crush their self-esteem, you're on the way to high stakes. But you're on the way to even higher, and better, stakes if you develop the protagonist in such a way that he is inherently likable, someone we want to reach into the pages of your book and shield from the cruel, cruel world.

A movie that elevated disappointment-based stakes masterfully was *Mystery, Alaska*. Mystery is a small, isolated town that lives, breathes, and bleeds hockey. Everyone in town grows up playing, and everyone in town aspires to make the Saturday game, which everyone else in town shows up to watch. The town council decides who makes the Saturday game...and whose time has come to retire (talk about an opportunity to crush a character's soul!). The town is so good at hockey that they often boast they could beat any team in the NHL. So when a man who grew up there—a man who was never very good at hockey and who left years ago for a journalism career in the big city—shows up back in Mystery with a film crew and the proposition that he'll nationally televise the boys of Mystery playing against the New York Rangers, the big game is on.

Now, we could stop there and ask *so what*: So what if the boys of Mystery lose to the Rangers when no one really expects them to win anyway? Disappointment, right? Sure, but a mistake in pitching *Mystery, Alaska* would be to stop there and conclude the pitch with something like this:

> Now the big game is on, and the boys of Mystery have only days to prepare. Will they put their

> money where their mouths are and defeat the Rangers? Or will they lose face on every TV screen in North America?

That's not particularly compelling, is it? All it does is restate the question that's already inherent in the setup. So even if your manuscript itself is rich with a colorful ensemble cast, and even if you've developed each character so that he has something unique at stake if Mystery loses the game—so that he stands to lose some part of himself, indeed, *a piece of his very soul*—this pitch doesn't do you any favors. It doesn't convey that wonderful depth of character that would be likely to hook an agent and make them request your full manuscript.

Now, another mistake—and I bring this up only because my example here features an ensemble cast—would be to pitch a laundry list of characters and what's at stake for each. You don't have enough real estate in your query letter for that; besides, laundry lists of *characters* in query pitches rarely tell us what we need to know about *story*. (I know. The balance is difficult to strike, but I never said this would be easy, did I?)

Mystery, Alaska is a classic underdog story. As such, it's set up from the first scene to make the audience cheer for Mystery. But…I'm going to spoil the ending now, so if you'd rather watch it yourself before reading the rest of this section, skip on ahead. The movie surprises us in a way few underdog stories do: Mystery loses the game. We expect them to win not because they're that good (they're playing the New York Rangers, after all), but because winning at the end is an expected trope of any underdog story. Yet in this story, one final slap shot, one last opportunity to tie the score as the clock ticks down to zero, hits the crossbar and bounces wide. So all the personal stakes, all the emotional jeopardy we were threatened with throughout the story, is about to bring each man to his knees…right?

Wrong. The difference is, in preparing for the game, each man has already confronted his own personal shortcomings and has grown internally, so the loss to the Rangers, while devastating, breaks none of them. In fact, as we see them standing proud on the ice at the end, we see that the loss, if anything, made them stronger.

Regardless of whether you cared for the movie, that is a masterful bit of emotional stakes building.

But there's another reason I like to talk about *Mystery, Alaska* when I talk about emotional stakes. There's a line of dialogue in this movie that gives us a very clear statement of stakes—something screenwriters do that once you recognize, you'll start seeing in every movie you watch. It's also something you might consider including in your own manuscripts. Here's the scene: Protagonist John (Russell Crowe) confronts Charlie (Hank Azaria), the man who brought the Rangers to Mystery and engineered the whole media circus surrounding the game. We already know these two were rivals back in the day and that Charlie carries a huge chip on his shoulder because he still feels like an outsider in his own hometown. Charlie, upset that no one has given him the pat on the back he expected for bringing the Rangers to town, asks, "What do I have to do? This town is hockey, hockey, hockey, right? So I bring back the New York Rangers."

John replies (and here is the statement of stakes), "You don't get it, do you? What if we lose this game? You brought back the one thing that could tear the heart out of this place."

Did you catch that? Not the one thing that could disappoint us or make us sad. *The one thing that could tear the heart out of this place.* With that simple statement, the screenwriter elevated the emotional stakes to the soul-crushing gut-punch that makes us, the audience, believe in fates worse than death.

And that's what your story's stakes must do for your readers. Get stakes on the page and make them clear in your pitch.

PUTTING IT ALL TOGETHER

If you've done the bookstore exercise; if you've identified and written down your novel's five W's; if you've jotted down a few sentences or clauses that start with *when, but, now, must, or else,* and *before*; and if you've followed along with how to hone the character, goal, motivation, conflict, and stakes parts of a pitch, then you're *almost* ready to write your pitch.

Almost?

Yes, almost. First, let's look at how to avoid common pitch pitfalls. *Then* you'll be ready.

PITCH PITFALLS

OMITTING CHARACTER, GOAL, MOTIVATION, CONFLICT, OR STAKES

We've just looked in great depth at the importance of crafting a pitch around the five W's: Who is your protagonist (character), what do they want (goal), why do they want it (motivation), why can't they have it (conflict), and what happens if they don't get it (stakes). So it's rather obvious that the first mistake is omitting one or more of these elements.

The concern is that the element is missing from your pitch because it's missing from your manuscript. Again, this is why it can be a valuable practice to write your pitch before you write your first draft. Otherwise, accept that if this happens to you, your manuscript might need another round of revisions. That's OK! Frustrating, yes, but it's so much better to have caught the problem now than to send out a manuscript that isn't ready and will likely be rejected.

To see if your query letter's pitch is solid, print it out and grab a highlighter. Highlight your protagonist's goal, motivation, stakes, and conflict. If they're all present and accounted for, you're on the right track!

"WATCH AS MY CHARACTER HAS ADVENTURES."

This type of statement worries me for two reasons. First, some of the most compelling fiction—and what acquiring editors are looking these days—is written in what we call deep or close point-of-view (POV). Whether in first person or third person, it's written in such a way that the reader is inside the POV character's head, behind the POV character's eyes, feeling what they feel, experiencing the story's events along with them. We are privy to the character's thoughts, emotions, and analyses.

A more distant POV plunks the reader down in the back row of the novel's proverbial theater. It separates us from the POV character. And it is often a reason agents and editors reject manuscripts. "I just didn't connect with the character(s)," their rejection letters say.

So when your query letter instructs me to "watch," I already have the sense that I'm not invited to be part of the story.

My second concern here is with the "as my character has adventures" bit. Characters having adventures is not story. Not if there's no structure to it. It sets me up for episodic storytelling at best and wandering, disconnected scenes at worst, so I'm already thinking a pitch that includes this directive is going to be a quick pass.

THE WANDERING PROTAGONIST

While we're on the topic of watching characters have adventures, I want to revisit something I mentioned briefly in the section on honing the goal part of your pitch. Let's revisit "along the way" and how it can lead to a problematic pitch. "Along the way" usually introduces a series of disjointed adventures, making it a phenomenon I've dubbed "the wandering protagonist." Here are three examples. See if you can discern why these pitches don't work.

Example 1: Middle-grade fantasy:

> Protagonist and his friends go on many exciting adventures. Along the way, they encounter a band of pirates, a herd of mystical unicorns, a swarm of angry fairies, and one club-swinging giant who just wants to find his way back to his home in the Mountains of Malforesia.

Example 2: Contemporary YA:

> It's the last summer before college, and in the

> wake of his father's death, Protagonist needs to figure out who he really is. He takes off on a cross-country road trip in Dad's old Jeep. Along the way, he meets a wise homeless man who teaches him about gratitude, a scrappy orphan who teaches him about forgiveness, and a blonde cocktail waitress who teaches him about love.

Example 3: Crime fiction:

> In her quest to capture a serial killer, Detective Protagonist must interview one quirky character after another: a past-her-prime exotic dancer who bakes the world's best chocolate-chip cookies, a grouchy old chess champion with an eidetic memory, and a cynical comedian whose dark sense of humor has managed to offend nearly everyone in Setting City.

In general, my question when I read an "along the way" query like this is, *along the way to what*? What happens at the end of the protagonist's journey? What were all the "exciting adventures" leading up to? Whatever it is, how did you set readers up for that in your manuscript's setup or first act? How does it all relate to the protagonist's internal conflict, to the growth and change they undergo (which is the whole point of story)? Do they obtain a skill, resource, or piece of information from each episodic adventure that at the climax, when they face off with the villain in some sort of epic final battle, will help them win?

Let's look at each example more closely.

In Example 1, our middle-grade protagonist has no goal—at least not one that's mentioned in the query letter. What does he want? What is he looking for? Why? What happens if he finds it, or doesn't? How can you make the reader care about Protagonist's impending success or failure? While this example does hint at conflict (pirates, angry fairies, a club-swinging giant), none of that conflict is directly hooked into the protagonist's goal. Do the angry fairies seek the same thing Protagonist seeks, and will they do anything to prevent him from getting it first? Are the pirates the swashbuckling sort, or are they another antagonistic force standing in Protagonist's way? Do our heroes end up helping the giant get back home? While the author might answer all that in the manuscript itself, this pitch, unfortunately, is too vague and does little to pique my interest.

In Example 2, we have a goal, but it's not a very strong one: Protagonist wants to find out who he really is. I'm concerned because that's the author pitching internal conflict. We're also missing motivation: Why does he need to find out who he really is (whatever that means), and what happens if he fails (stakes)? We are given hints of conflict: He's mourning the death of his father, and apparently, he needs to learn about gratitude, forgiveness, and love. But in this example both goal and conflict are internal to the protagonist. Remember that there are two kinds of dramatic conflict—internal and external—and that a good story develops both. Give this protagonist an external goal (to visit his grandmother in Sedona, to scatter is father's ashes at Niagara Falls, to return something his father stole to its rightful owner, etc.) and some external conflict (the Jeep keeps breaking down, the scrappy orphan steals his wallet, his sister is chasing him across the country to stop him from returning the object their father stole, etc.).

In sum, while the protagonist goes places, does stuff, meets people, and even learns a few important life lessons along the way, *that is not story*—at least not in the way that agents, editors, and publishers working in commercial fiction define story. Hollywood's the same. Story in commercial-fiction and entertainment spaces includes a traceable throughline. It starts with a question and ends with an answer *to that question*, not some different question that popped up *along the way*. The story question boils down to goal: Will the protagonist achieve it or not?

In Example 3, we have a goal that's both clear and genre appropriate: to capture a serial killer. The motivation is implied: to stop the killer from killing again. The stakes are also implied: If Detective Protagonist fails, someone else will die. So far so good, though for higher, better stakes, make the killer's next target someone close to Detective Protagonist. Make the stakes personal! But after that, this pitch gets lost in wandering-protagonist territory, and the rest of it contains zero conflict.

The wandering-protagonist pitch is often crafted as an attempt to hook the agent on its sheer quirkiness. And the manuscript might be an utter joy to read! There's nothing wrong with a novel in which the main character goes on a journey, and anyone on a journey is bound to meet interesting folks, human or otherwise, along the way. However, journeys and interesting side characters alone are not quite story and not quite plot. So avoid the wandering, along-the-way protagonist when pitching your story. It might sap your chances of getting your manuscript requested.

QUOTING YOUR CHARACTERS

I've read many a pitch in which the author quotes a line of dialogue directly from their novel, something poignant or cool one of their characters says that the author feels really encapsulates something thematically important about the book as a whole. I'd recommend you not do this, simply because, again, your pitch should give us the 30,000-foot view of your story. Giving us a line (or more) of dialogue verbatim sinks us into a particular moment, which is disorienting because we're not familiar with the larger landscape to which that moment relates. It's like trying to sell a particular make and model of a car by leading with the plushiness of the upholstery. Focus on the macro in your pitch, not the micro.

DESCRIBING ONE SCENE IN GREAT DETAIL

Similarly, do not waste space in your pitch describing one particular scene. This is a big mistake I see in a lot of query letters. All writers have pet scenes in their novels—scenes that made them cry, cheer, or bite their nails as they wrote them, scenes that developed something important or emotionally poignant about a favorite character. But pitching one scene alone will not sell your book. In fact, pitching a single scene might make an agent worry that your story doesn't have a solid throughline. Poorly structured novels are difficult to pitch well, so the assumption might be that you're pitching a really good scene to compensate.

PITCHING INTERNAL CONFLICT

I'd estimate that well over half—maybe even closer to three-quarters—of the query pitches I read, or the pitches I take face-to-face at conferences, include some variation of the phrase "which forces the protagonist to figure out who she really is."

That in itself is not a problem. After all, your protagonist should have an internal arc, right? How else are you going to demonstrate how they grew and changed as a result of your story's external events? As far as internal arcs go, identity crisis or identity emergence are pretty universal, so you could do worse.

The problem is when writers deliver a pitch that's focused so tightly on the protagonist's internal journey that I'm left with little or no sense or understanding of the story. Let's look at an example:

> I've written a 90,000-word adult science-fiction novel about a tax attorney named Tim who enlists in the Intergalactic Army to defend Earth from aliens. It's about the nature of leadership and sacrifice, and throughout the course of the book, Tim will be forced to become courageous and discover who he really is.

The first sentence was awesome! But then...really? You wrote 90,000 words about leadership, sacrifice, and a middle-aged guy discovering himself? I don't even know what that means. But I'm already bored. Try this instead:

> I've written a 90,000-word adult science-fiction novel about a shy, quiet tax attorney named Tim. When Tim's wife and daughter are killed in the first wave of an alien attack on earth (inciting incident, motivation), he's left with nothing to lose. He enlists in the Intergalactic Army—if he's going to die, too, he's going to die fighting (goal, character

> development). But Tim hasn't done a push-up in years, and the last time he played racquetball with his boss, he suffered a major asthma attack (conflict, more character development). He's not the ideal soldier, but neither are all the other men and women in his unit. Earth, after all, doesn't have many ideal soldiers left (world building). When his commanding officer is captured during the second wave (rising action), Tim must lead the surviving members of his unit on a treacherous mission (stakes) to rescue her (external goal)... even if it means he must make the ultimate sacrifice (rising stakes, intriguing hook).

In our revised pitch, you do not need the words "Tim will have to discover who he really is" or "Tim will have to discover what he's really made of." Those phrases mean nothing. The internal arc is inherent because the pitch begins with words like *shy, quiet, asthma,* and *not ideal,* and it concludes with words like *lead, surviving, treacherous mission, rescue,* and *ultimate sacrifice.* Let the pitch itself do the work of communicating the internal arc.

ALL WORLD OR NO WORLD

I mentioned in the section on honing the character part of your pitch that some queries neglect to mention a protagonist. These are often pitches for science fiction, fantasy, or historical novels where the author is, perhaps subconsciously, more impressed by their own world building or research than they are with their actual story, and they're hoping an agent will be, too.

But just as often, we see queries that don't mention any world details at all, or they mention a few world details that clash, preventing us from fully understanding the story's milieu. For instance, if a query mentions corsets in one sentence and iPhones in the next, I'm confused. Either your present-day character has a cool, vintage fashion sense, or you've imagined an alternate-history world, or world in which time-travel is possible. In any case, it is definitely worth devoting a sentence or two of your pitch to preemptively clearing that up.

Ask a friend who's unfamiliar with your manuscript to read your pitch, and then ask them for their impressions of your novel's setting (time and place, real or imagined). Avoid writing a blank-slate pitch, which makes it seem as though your story could take place in present-day New Jersey as easily as it could take place nineteenth-century England. The key here is to either state the time and place clearly at the beginning of your pitch or evoke your story world with well-chosen details laced into the pitch itself and use era-appropriate vocabulary and phrasing.

TOO MANY MADE-UP WORDS

Agent Kristin and I used to run query-letter webinars. Registrants would submit their query letters ahead of time, and then during the webinar, I would read each query out loud, and Agent Kristin would stop me when she, if she were reading that query in the slush pile, would stop reading. Then she'd do a detailed critique, looking closely at where each query lost her and what each writer could do to improve their chances of getting a full-manuscript request. (We haven't offered that webinar in a long time—we should do it again!)

For me as the reader, the queries for fantasy projects were the worst. Fantasy writers do a lot of name generation, and in some of those queries, it seemed like every other word was weirdly heavy on consonants, vowels, syllables, hyphens, accent marks, impossible-to-pronounce phonemes, or apostrophes. (Apostrophes! Whoever decided that apostrophes are the best way to indicate that a name is fantastical or otherworldly should have patented the idea.) I would struggle through the pronunciations as best I could, but Agent Kristin never made it to the end of these queries. Not only were they making *me* work too hard, but even if I were able to pronounce each made-up word perfectly and without pause, they were making *her* work too hard, too. Anyone reading that type of query, out loud or silently to themselves, has to slow way down to figure out by context clues alone if every made-up word is the name of a person, place, or thing. And anything that slows an agent down when they have some hundred or more queries to read every day before they can get back to that contract or client edit is likely to get a quick pass.

This isn't a question of dumbing down your pitch. It's common sense. Reading a query letter and reading a novel are two very different types of reading that involve different parts of the brain. When reading queries, agents have to read fast while passing each through their own filters and evaluating each on a number of criteria. On the other hand, when an agent is reading a novel, they slow down like any other reader does, suspending their disbelief, letting the writer introduce them to the story world, and savoring how the story unfolds for the characters.

Don't let your query get too thick, fancy, or esoteric, regardless of how cerebral or elevated your manuscript might be. Write your query to be clear, to be read and understood quickly. Don't give agents an excuse to give up before they even begin.

"HAVE YOU EVER WONDERED...?"

Many authors open their query letters with a question or directive intended to get the agent to step inside the novel's world or premise. "Have you ever wondered...?" gets used a lot, as does "What would you do if...?" We also see "Imagine a world...," "Picture this...," and "Allow me to transport you to...."

I encourage you to cut these types of phrases from your query. Not only are they awkward and gimmicky, but they're a waste of real estate. If your pitch is strong enough, then the agent will automatically imagine or picture your world. They'll automatically feel transported. They'll automatically wonder what they would do if they were in your protagonist's shoes. So focus on making your pitch strong enough to stand on its own without your needing to set the agent up for it or issue an invitation.

VAGUE, AMBIGUOUS, AND OVERUSED WORDS AND PHRASES

Along those lines, here is a list of words and phrases to avoid in your query letter. They are overused, overly fancy, ambiguous, or cliché.

- *So begins the story of...* This is most often used immediately after an author has introduced their pitch with a detailed description or direct quote from an early scene in their manuscript—again, not something I'd recommend you do, as your pitch should give us a wide view of your story and not get too specific about any particular scene.
- *This is her story...* This is often offered as the final line of a pitch, and it feels a bit dramatic, like it's supposed to be a big reveal or the period on the end of a sentence. If the query reader gets to the

end of your pitch and is still reading, then they should already know whose story this is without the writer's having to clarify.

- *Unbeknownst to her...* The word "unbeknownst" is fancy-talk for "she doesn't know." If it's a word you don't use in regular speech (in an unironic sense), and it's a word your characters wouldn't use, then think about why you're using it in your pitch.
- *Turning her world upside down* or *her world is turned upside down...* This is vague and cliché. Of course your character's world is going to be turned upside down. That's what story is. Instead, get specific. Rather than "When Mary finds out her husband is cheating on her, her world turns upside down," try "When Mary finds out her husband is cheating on her, she kicks him out of the house." Whenever possible, pitch the action instead of the emotional beat. Many, many query pitches lean into the vague emotional beats, leaving query readers with little to no understanding of whether there's an actual story on the page.
- *Her world is shattered...* Vague and cliché, this is another emotional-beat phrase. See above.
- *She must pick up the pieces...* See above.
- *Forced to question everything she thought she knew*

or *everything she thought she knew was a lie...* See above.

- *Shocked to discover...* Cliché.
- *She must embark on a journey...* This is similar to "turning her world upside down" in that all story is journey, whether an internal, emotional journey of growth and change or a literal journey from one place to another. Worse, it's ambiguous. If you're pitching a middle-grade fantasy, then change "embarking on a journey" to something that evokes adventure, and be specific: "She must travel by airship, submersible, and unicorn to the fabled land of Malforesia." If you're pitching a thriller, change "she must embark on a journey" to something that evokes danger and tension, and, again, be specific: "For days, she stalks the killer, following him from the dark alleys of Detroit to the frozen shores of Hudson Bay."
- *He is hell-bent on* or *he is dead-set on...* "Hell-bent" and "dead-set" are clichés. They probably show up in every third query I read, maybe more. Be fresh!
- *Evil will be unleashed...* "Unleashed" is cliché.
- *She will stop at nothing...* Vague and cliché.
- *He must unlock the mystery* or *he must solve the mystery...* Overused.

- *She turns the tables* or *the tables are turned...* Vague and cliché.
- *Along the way...* I've already discussed this phrase above, in the section about the wandering protagonist. But it belongs in this list, too, since it's a seductive little cliché that can derail your pitch.
- *As events unfold* or *as the story unfolds...* In a pitch, this is often a shortcut to get the query reader from A to B. It's the "stuff happens" shortcut. But can you be more specific? Instead of "as events unfold, she comes to realize her world has been shattered," try "as her husband moves out and their only son leaves for college, she realizes she's alone for the first time in her life."
- *A chain of events...* See above.
- *In the process...* See above.

CLUTTER WORDS

On the subject of words and phrases to avoid in your query letter, here's a second category. I separated this list from the previous one because these aren't vague, ambiguous, or overused. Well, they *are* overused, but not in the sense that they have become query clichés. I call the following clutter words because they invariably lead to unnecessarily cluttered, wordy pitches. So if you've already written your pitch, stop here, print it out, and circle any instances of the following clutter words:

> character, main character, hero, protagonist, antagonist, villain, bad guy, narrator, plot, narrative, set, setting, world, style, voice, point of view, description, dialogue, scene, theme

These are the elements of fiction, much like *line, shape, color, value, texture,* and *space* are the elements of art. Now circle any instances of the following as well:

> book, novel, story, follows, transports, focuses on, is geared to, centers around, is aimed at, opens, begins, ends, ending, conclusion, twist, readers

Why are clutter words problematic? Let's look at some examples of how they can lead to a cluttered a pitch:

- The **main character** of my **book**, Jane Smith, is a sixteen-year-old-girl who…
- **Readers** will **follow my protagonist**, sixteen-year-old Jane Smith, as she…
- The **novel opens** with Jane Smith, age sixteen…
- The **plot** of my **story centers around** sixteen-year-old Jane Smith and **opens** with a **scene** in which she…
- Told from the **point of view** of my sixteen-year-old **narrator**, Jane Smith, this **book**…
- This **story** about a teen **heroine** named Jane Smith **is aimed at readers** between the ages of…

I read dozens of queries every day in which the pitch leads off in a similar fashion. The problem is, every one of them can be reworded, or *decluttered*, as follows:

Sixteen-year-old Jane Smith…

Yes, it really is that simple. Five words. Tack Jane's goal or the inciting incident onto the end of that sentence, and your pitch is off to a solid start. Character. Goal. Motivation. Conflict. Stakes. Boom. Let's look at some other examples of cluttered query phrasing:

- The lush **setting** of my **novel** is really a **character** in and of itself…
- Through my unique **style** and **voice**, my use of beautiful **description**, and my finely crafted **narrative**, I **transport** the **reader** to a **world** where startling **plot twists**…
- The witty **dialogue** between the **hero** and **villain** will keep **readers** laughing as they turn the **pages** toward the unexpected **conclusion**…

In 99% of queries I read, this kind of thing is 100% unnecessary. It's dangerous to devote your query letter's valuable real estate to pitching the elements of fiction instead of, well, just pitching your fiction. Get to the story! Remember: Editors in the commercial-fiction space buy books based on memorable characters, and on plots driven by conflict and tension. The elements of fiction are important to your craft, but they don't tell a slush reader much about what's actually happening on the page.

Let's go back to Jane Smith. This time we'll not only declutter a clunky pitch lead-in, but we'll also start crafting a more focused, plot-specific pitch:

> This novel focuses on themes of redemption and forgiveness by following young protagonist Jane Smith as she comes of age during the Depression…

Let's declutter thusly, with a focus on plot:

> As Jane Smith comes of age during the Depression, [insert goal, inciting incident, motivation, and stakes]…

But what about redemption and forgiveness? Is it really a bad idea to mention themes in a query letter? Not necessarily. But if you do feel it's necessary to talk theme, avoid being vague. This is vague:

> As Jane Smith comes of age during the Depression, she's forced to make tough choices that will have long-standing consequences on her future, ultimately leading her to learn about redemption and forgiveness…

In this example, there are no elements of fiction mentioned—yay!—but, frankly, it's the type of sentence my eyes would skip right over in a query. I'm looking for story. What "tough choices" do you force poor Jane

Smith to make? What are the "consequences" and how do they make Jane's situation even worse? What does Jane do that forces her to seek "redemption and forgiveness"? Instead, try this:

> As Jane Smith comes of age during the Depression, she's forced to choose between a California dairy-farm job that will help feed her seven younger sisters and the love of a boy whose promise to whisk her away to India leads her to betray her family in the time of their greatest need. When she returns from the East six months later…

Now we're talking! Here's the start of a clear, specific query pitch that focuses on character and plot—and there's not a single element of fiction in sight!

It's time. Go forth confidently and write your pitch! Remember, just like writing a novel, you don't have to (and probably shouldn't) settle for your first draft. Give yourself some latitude to write more than one version and see which one feels best. Once you're happy with your pitch, you're ready to add the bio to the end, and your query letter will, at last, be complete.

CHAPTER 8

THE FOUR-PART QUERY LETTER

PART FOUR: THE BIO

THIS FOURTH AND FINAL PART OF THE QUERY LETTER causes a lot of stress among writers new to the query process. What can you say about yourself that will impress an agent? That will make you come across as professional, but also friendly and approachable, amicable and hardworking? If you have a lot of credentials, how do you pack it all in without sounding cocky? Worse, what if you're relatively new to this and don't yet have any credentials at all?

I'm here to tell you that you don't need a bunch of shiny credentials to secure an agent's representation. Remember how I said (over and over again, actually) that your query letter is all about your pitch? Well, it is. If you have a good story idea that's well written, you'll pique interest. Stay focused on that.

I'm also here to tell you that you probably have credentials you don't realize you have—positives that are definitely worth mentioning in the bio section of your query letter. So take heart. Here's where to look for and what to include.

PREVIOUS PUBLICATIONS

Obviously, if you've had books published in the past, you'll want to mention that. If it's a lot of books, please don't list them all. Mention one or two the agent is most likely to have heard of, and then invite the agent to visit your website to view your complete backlist. Maybe you had a bestseller break big and earn glowing reviews from major outlets (*Kirkus, Publishers Weekly, School Library Journal, New York Times, USA Today,* etc.) or solid sales (keeping in mind we can look up your book's point-of-sale numbers on BookScan so this isn't the place you want to stretch the truth). That's a book you want to mention.

Who your publisher was matters, too. If you had a book published by a Big Five or other large, established house like Sourcebooks or Houghton Mifflin Harcourt, that's a title to mention. You might even say who your editor was.

If you don't have any of that but you did have a book

published by a small press, great! Tell us! If you don't have a novel published, but you did have a short story accepted here or a poem accepted there, go ahead and throw that in your bio. What if you had an article published in some obscure online science journal about the effects of houseplants on mood? Great! If you have no fiction pubs to mention, then mention your other published writings. Heck, mention that you write a column for your company's internal newsletter.

All of this tells me you're writing and submitting, which tells me that you have at least some measure of thickness to your skin, you've been through the editorial process, and you have experience writing for an audience. It tells me that even though this might be your first novel, you are already doing what Professional Writers do.

PRIOR REPRESENTATION

If you have previous publications with a larger house, then chances are you had prior representation as well, since most larger houses and their many imprints don't accept submissions by unagented authors. Prior rep is also something to mention in your bio even if your last agent left the biz or you parted ways before they took your manuscript out on submission.

You don't have to confess everything about that relationship here. You don't even have to say who your prior agent was. However, if the agent you're querying is interested enough in your pitch to call you up and have a conversation, then that's the time to be forthcoming. If your prior agent was well known and highly respected, then telling us who it was in your query letter will definitely make us sit up and pay closer attention to your pitch. But even if it wasn't a big-name agent, mentioning that you had prior rep tells us you've been active in the industry before now, which means you know something about how the game is played, and you might be likely to have more realistic expectations about the journey ahead.

Let's take a little side trip here and talk about what to do if you currently have an agent but want a different one. If you're in the market for a new agent, no matter your reason, sever ties with your existing agent before shopping for a new one. For an agent, finding out that one of their author-clients is sneaking around and looking to replace them is hurtful and confusing, and it could cause them to drop you preemptively. If your response to that is, "I don't care, I was going to leave anyway," then why didn't you? Agents know each other, and they talk, so assume any behind-the-back dealings on your part will be discovered—and in no scenario will you come out looking good. Worse than the hurt party's emotional response is that such behavior borders on unethical and could make the idea of working with you unappealing to others in the field. Yes, it's scary for an agented writer to suddenly be unagented, but just as you shouldn't cheat on your life partner, you shouldn't cheat on your agent. Sever the relationship first, then look for new representation.

That said, know that agent-author partnerships dissolve all the time. Maybe you parted ways under the best of circumstances or your agent left the business, so now you're looking for new representation. How should you address that in your query letter?

As soon as you find yourself without representation, it doesn't hurt to contact the agents on your wish list. First, share a little about your situation. You don't have to go into any great detail about the nature of the split, but expect any prospective agent to get on the phone with your former agent and ask them what it was like working with you. It's no different from a prospective employer chatting with your last boss or other professional references to find out more about you before deciding whether to extend you an offer.

Your wording in your query letter might be as simple as "My agent and I have parted ways and I am looking for new representation." Some writers refer to an "amicable split." That's good. It's always nice for a prospective agent to know that your prior professional relationship ended, well, *professionally*, with minimal drama or contention.

If you wish, it's OK to *briefly* explain the nature of the

split. Perhaps you wanted to branch out into new genres that your former agent didn't represent, or, as already mentioned, perhaps the agent has left the business (which happens frequently).

What you *don't* want to do here is complain. No digs about how your former agent failed you. I don't care if they stuck you in revision hell for years and never took your book out on submission. I don't care if they made promises to you they never kept. I don't care if they ignored your calls, withheld payments, or faked offers from nonexistent publishers. I don't even care if their ouster from the Association of Authors Representatives just got splashed all over the cover of *Publishers Weekly*. Your query letter is not the place to air dirty laundry—yours or anyone else's. That approach just makes *you* look bad. Conversations about how you've been burned and what you can reasonably expect from your new agent should happen *only after* your prospective agent has responded to your query with a desire to learn more about you, your body of work, or your next project.

Speaking of your next project: If you're looking for new representation, it's best if you have a new, completed project for your new agent to shop. Depending on the agency agreement you signed with your former agent, your former agent most likely has the right to continue earning their commission on all book contracts they negotiated on your behalf, for the life of those contracts—that is, until the publisher officially declares the books on those contracts out of print.

That means your backlist provides no direct financial benefit for your new agent. Indirectly, your new agent will only benefit from your backlist insofar as (a) they are legally free to sell any available (unsold) subsidiary rights to your already published books, and (b) you've racked up an impressive readership that will follow you to your future books or series. So having something new to pitch will work in your favor.

EDUCATION, EXPERIENCE, AND AWARDS RELATIVE TO WRITING

If you have a degree, certificate, major, or minor in some area of language arts, that should appear in your bio. Have an MFA in creative writing? Even better…maybe. One thing I've learned after reading so many queries, sample chapters, and manuscripts over the years is this: Earning an MFA might make someone a better writer than they were before they entered their program, but on the whole, writers with MFAs don't necessarily stand out in the slush pile. In fact, some writers with MFAs have a tough time transitioning from writing for professors, fellow MFA students, and literary mags to writing commercial novels for popular-fiction audiences. That said, earning your

MFA is a feat worth mentioning in your query letter. My point is, if you don't have one, don't feel like you need to rush out and get one, because you absolutely do not.

I mentioned earlier that if you have any writing experience at all, that's material for your bio. Do you contribute to a parenting blog? Edit your small-town newspaper's op-ed section? Write marketing copy for a shoe company? Awesome. That's you putting words on paper. That's you building your credentials. That's you participating in Professional Writer behavior.

Any awards, nominations, or contest recognition you've earned for your writing (making the finals, earning an honorable mention, or, of course, winning) are other things worth mentioning in your bio. Did you win a spot in a well-regarded mentorship program like Pitch Wars? That will get an agent's attention! However, if the recognition was *for the novel you're querying*, then fold that into your query letter's project summary. If the recognition was *for some other piece of writing*, then mention it here, in your bio.

EDUCATION OR EXPERIENCE RELATIVE TO YOUR NOVEL'S SUBJECT

OK, what if you really, truly, honestly have none of the above? No past pubs, no prior rep, no professional writing experience, and no language-arts degree, so definitely no writing-related awards or recognition?

Then trust me: If your pitch and sample are solid, you're still in the running.

The next place to look for bio material is in your non-writing-related credentials—especially if they're related to your novel's subject or protagonist's profession. Are you pitching a police procedural, and you spent sixteen years as a cop? Boom. Tell me that, and I'm already going into your sample pages with elevated trust in your voice and expertise. Are you a litigator pitching a legal drama? A volunteer coroner pitching a mystery that's going to be heavy on the medical forensics? Are you a special-education teacher writing about a kid with autism? A forest ranger writing a survival story set in the wilderness? A widow writing about grief? A stand-up comic writing humor? An athlete writing about characters who play your particular sport? A chef writing about a quirky cast of restaurant employees? You get the picture.

Establishing this type of experience assures an agent that your story will be authentic. You are, or have been, part of your protagonist's world, so you have an insider's perspective on the conflicts that tend to arise as well as their available solutions. You know what standard operating procedures would be required of your characters and what consequences they'd face for stepping outside those bounds. You know the types of personalities your particular milieu attracts, so your characters will feel more authentic too, especially to readers who share your expertise. And readers who don't will feel immersed in something new.

OK, but what if you don't have this type of connection with your novel either? You're a land-locked American who majored in business and marketing, but your novel is about an Italian yacht captain who saves thirty-six refugees from a rubber raft in the Mediterranean?

Guess what? Don't sweat it! At the end of the day, this is fiction. If you've done your research (about Italy, boats, maritime law, international asylum policy, and the ways in which trauma manifests in refugees, etc.) and you've written a good book about compelling characters, you're still gold. Focus on that pitch.

That said, in your query letter, feel free to use the adjective "well-researched," if you must, but stop there. Avoid the urge to expound. I've read many a query that goes on and on about all the research the author did—not to mention many a manuscript that reads not like a novel, but like a walkthrough of all the author's research. And I get it: The more a person researches something (a place, a time, a culture), the more they fall in love with it and the more they want others to fall in love with it, too, so it's easy to let research shove its way to the front. But think of your research like an iceberg: underneath the surface is the huge body of knowledge you had to amass before you could select the maybe 10% or so that actually gets to appear in your story.

In sum, of course you researched. That should go without saying. Researching is part of the job of Professional Writer. Pitching your research in your query letter is not going to tip the scales in your favor. A well-researched book that's poorly written is still poorly written. It won't sell, no matter how much research you did.

The bottom line is, it's still interesting to know who you are in your non-writing life. If you're a banker, plumber, stay-at-home parent, college student, retired orthopedic surgeon, or whatever else, tell us. A little snippet about who you are is humanizing, and that's refreshing in a process like querying that can feel terribly cursory and impersonal.

PROFESSIONAL MEMBERSHIPS

If you are a member of any national or international writing organization, that should go in your bio. There is a professional organization for nearly every top-level commercial genre: International Thriller Writers (ITW), Mystery Writers of America (MWA), Society for Children's Book Writers and Illustrators (SCBWI),

Romance Writers of America (RWA), Horror Writers Association (HWA), Science Fiction and Fantasy Writers of America (SFWA), and Women's Fiction Writers Association (WFWA), to name a few. Many have regional chapters that offer educational programming, critique groups, networking events, and other opportunities to join a community of like-minded creatives. In addition, most hold annual conferences where writers can meet bestselling authors and attend workshops and panels on the practice of writing and business of publishing. These conferences are also attended by agents and editors who are there to take pitch appointments—so if writing query letters isn't your cup of tea, sign up for pitch appointments at these types of conferences.

Other regional organizations that are not genre-specific offer similar types of events and opportunities. Here on Colorado's Front Range are Rocky Mountain Fiction Writers, Pikes Peak Writers, Northern Colorado Writers, and Lighthouse Writers Workshop, among others. If you're a member of a regional org like this, definitely mention that in your bio. Again, this sort of thing tells us that you're part of the writing community. You're in the know. You're not holed up alone in your attic writing novels that the agent you're querying will be the first person to read.

By the way, most organizations and their chapters

hold contests, and the entry fee for a lot of these contests includes a written critique of your entry. If a critique is not included, it might be offered for a small upcharge. Either way, contests that include critiques are another fantastic way to get anonymous feedback on your work and start thickening your skin. No, you're absolutely not going to love everything a judge has to say about your writing. Cry and rage in private, then take a deep breath, open your mind, and see if the judge doesn't have a point or two. At the end of the day, you will have a very tough time in this industry if your ego bruises easily. You'll have a tougher time still if you rage about such things out loud or on social media. Be cool. Guard your reputation fiercely, even as a pre-published author. Professionalism matters.

And maybe you will love what the judges have to say. You just might walk away from a contest with a finalist ribbon, a cash-prize win...or an offer of representation or publication. That's right. Many contests ask agents and acquiring editors to serve as final-round judges. I have several friends here in Denver's writing community whose participation in a contest launched their career. You'll never know unless you enter.

OTHER WRITING-RELATED ACTIVITIES

If being a Professional Writer is what you really want to

do, then I would highly recommend that you invest in a membership to a reputable writing organization and that you attend some kind of large-scale writing conference at least once per year. Expensive? Yes. But it's an investment in your desired career.

That said, I also understand such things are not within everyone's reach. What can you do instead? Join a critique group that meets in person or online. Attend writing lectures or workshops at your local bookstore, library, cultural-arts center, or community college. Find a mentor, an established writer willing to work with you one-on-one, or apply for one of the reputable mentorship programs out there, like Pitch Wars or Author Mentor Match. Get your stuff out there. Be a joiner. Invite other writers into your writing world. Any way you are already doing that is fair game for your query letter's bio.

BIO PITFALLS

ARROGANCE OR AGGRESSIVENESS

Few things will turn an agent off faster than a tone of arrogance—or, worse, aggression—in a query letter. I think a lot of folks who employ this tactic believe they are being *confident*. But instead, what often happens is that they come off as uninformed, even silly.

One phrase that pops up in the slush pile every so often is "I am the next [insert bestselling author]." As much as we'd love to believe that, we just don't. We've read enough slush to believe otherwise. Unfortunately, 99.9 times out of 100, the pitch and sample that accompany a claim like this are miles from bestseller status, and on the .1% chance that the submission really is outstanding, the tone of the query has already soured our stomachs. Further, this claim demonstrates a lack of respect for the years of sweat and toil that whichever bestselling author you're comparing yourself to put in to mastering their craft before they achieved their status.

Here's another one: "If you don't represent me, you'll be making a huge mistake." These are the same writers who tend to respond to form rejections with snide comments like "your loss" or "you'll be sorry" or "you just turned your back on an easy $1,000,000." So sure are they of their inevitable success in an industry that assures no one of anything, ever, that their expectations—nay, their *demands*—are already so high, so unrealistic, as to be laughable. Most agents roll their eyes and click right past queries like this.

There's a slightly more cheerful tone to things like "let's join forces and make a ton of money." Maybe such things are meant to be tongue-in-cheek, but really, they're just as goofy. The expectations and general lack of understanding about what it takes for anyone in this industry (agents and editors included) to make "a ton of money" are enough to make a query that includes this sort of phrase an easy pass. (Here's a longstanding industry joke: How do you make a small fortune in publishing? You start with a large fortune.)

Another thing that comes off as arrogant, not to mention uninformed, is when self-published authors who are seeking a traditional deal write their query letters with strings attached. They say things like, "My last self-published trilogy netted me X-amount of money. If you can guarantee me at least X-percent more than that for this trilogy, I'll allow you to shop it." Or they put forth odd and unrealistic terms that sound a little like back-alley mafia dealings: "I'm going to make you a deal you can't refuse, and you are one of only a handful of agents I'm approaching with this offer, so act fast. Here it is: You sign me. I keep all print, ebook, and audio rights. You sell translation and movie rights, and we'll split those earnings fifty-fifty."

This is where I hear the sound bite from that Geico commercial in my head, the one with the woman showing her friends all the Polaroids taped to her living room wall because she doesn't understand that social media "walls" exist online. Her friend tells her, "That's not how it works. That's now how any of this works."

The thing is, self-publishing is totally legit, and if you as a self-published author are satisfied with your reach and income, then a lot of agents are going to wonder why you're querying them in the first place. If you want to become a hybrid author—an author who self-publishes here and writes for traditional publishing houses there—that is also legit. But your best bet when developing the traditional side of your career is to approach agents with an understanding of what agents do under which terms, and how traditional publishing works.

I once taught a workshop at a fairly large conference. After my workshop, a writer who had been in the audience followed me out into the hall, told me about his self-publishing successes, and then demanded that I "pitch an agent's services" to him. He actually told me to *pitch him*, to sell him on why he would bother to look for agent representation. "What can an agency do for me that I can't already do for myself?" he ordered me to tell him.

I can answer that question. In fact, I did in my book *Do You Need a Literary Agent?* The answer is, it depends on what your goals are—which was about the extent of my response in this particular situation before we shifted to a more pleasant and neutral topic on our way to the conference luncheon. I would have been happy to discuss an agent's role further if I'd gotten the sense that he honestly didn't know what agents do. But industry folks recognize gatekeeper resentment when we see it, and we're confronted with it regularly. There are a lot of writers out there who are angry that agents exist and are still part of the system. That resentment grows with every rejection a writer receives, and it can seep into the tone and phrasing of query letters.

If you've been around the query block a time or two already, then have a friend read your letter for tone. There may be opportunities for you to smooth it out a bit, both in what you say and how you say it.

MENTIONING TV OR MOVIE RIGHTS

Never mention TV or movie rights in your query letter. Really. Don't. It puts the cart before the horse (step one: sell your novel), but it also demonstrates that your expectations are uncalibrated. Even if you say something like, "I'm a very visual writer so I think my work would translate well to the big screen," my red flag will start climbing the pole.

We at Nelson Literary Agency always negotiate hard with publishers to retain TV and movie rights on our clients' behalf because we'll get you, and us, more money if we sell those rights ourselves. And we sell *a lot* of TV and movie options to our clients' books with the help of our entertainment attorneys and co-agents. Most options go for a few thousand dollars, making them a nice little bump for the author but not nearly as lucrative as aspiring novelists imagine. Options expire after a year or two. At that point, we'll either renegotiate your option, shop the rights to other companies, or, if Hollywood interest has waned, simply let the option expire.

So how many of these deals actually get turned into movies?

Well, Nelson Literary Agency was founded in 2002, and our first movie—that is, the first film adapted from one of our client's books—got made in 2018. That was *Bird Box*, produced by Netflix based on the novel of the same name by Josh Malerman. Other agencies' mileages may vary, but one film in sixteen years—across four agents, hundreds of clients, thousands of novels, and oodles of film and TV options—is pretty dang good.

That's the reality, and it's what I mean when I say that an author who mentions movie rights in their query letter has uncalibrated expectations. Know that film and TV rights, as well as stage-play rights, exist in every standard publishing contract, so that river will be crossed when you come to it. But you can't get to that river until you sell your novel.

Another phrase I see in query letters once in a while is, "I already have Netflix/HBO/Amazon Prime on board to do the movie version." That's a tough one to believe. First, if a writer already has signatures from

Big Fancy Movie Company, then it's BFMC or their attorneys who are contacting us, probably through our own entertainment attorney or co-agents, not the writer. Furthermore, if a writer sold the performance rights to *a draft of their unpublished novel* to BFMC *without an agent* (are you hearing how that sounds?), then (a) they got completely taken advantage of during the negotiation and don't even know it, so there's probably not much value to an agent jumping in at this point, and (b) BFMC would most likely take the writer's idea and hire someone else to write the script, and then hire someone *else* to write the novelization of that script, cutting the writer out completely.

That's not to say that Cinderella stories don't exist—self-published, un-agented authors who have achieved significant sales and followings do get approached by Hollywood scouts, and deals have been inked. The difference is, these authors *have achieved significant sales.* I'm far more likely to take seriously a claim that lays out this sort of situation than I am a similar claim from a previously unpublished author.

Another claim we see on occasion is, "Name Drop at BFMC has expressed interest in TV/movie rights to my novel, but they suggested I secure agent representation and sell the book first, so I'm reaching out to you." OK, sure. That's a plausible scenario, and I'll treat this query the same way I'll treat any query—which is to say, I'll read the pitch with an eye toward whether this is a novel one of our agents would be excited to represent and able to sell. But at the back of my mind will be the maxim I once heard a film-industry person relay at a conference: "When anyone in Hollywood gushes about your novel, fawns over you, tells you how amazing and thrilling your premise is and how you're sure the next big thing, that feels pretty awesome. But in Hollywood speak, all they really just said to you is hello."

It's not quite the same in publishing, obviously, so wires get crossed and misunderstandings occur. My initial directive to never, ever mention movie or TV rights in your query letter carries one caveat: If you know for sure that you have solid, legitimate interest in your work and you're willing to name names so that we can reach out for verification, that's when it's appropriate to mention these rights in your query.

TOO MUCH RÉSUMÉ OR CV

This is simply a real-estate issue. Your query letter is not a résumé or curriculum vitae, where you lay out all the jobs you've held or all the career-related experience you've racked up. Remember that the bulk your query letter should be your pitch. When your pitch and bio are the same length—or worse, when your bio is longer than your pitch, which is something I see daily—you've mishandled your query letter's real estate. You've missed the opportunity to pitch the heck out of your book.

Again: The purpose of your query letter is to sell your book. So keep that bio tight and relevant.

"WHY I WRITE" DISCLOSURES

Writers are artists. They're passionate about what they do. They'd better be, because writing is grueling work, and the publishing industry can look like a cold, doorless, windowless tower to those looking for a way in. However, I get a little nervous when I'm reading a query letter that includes "why I write" or "why I wrote this book" narratives.

The most common is this: "I am passionate about writing. It's the only thing I ever wanted to do. I've been writing stories since I learned how to hold a pencil." There's nothing wrong with this type of thing per se, but ask yourself: Does it do anything to sell your book? No. Does it do anything to help you stand out in the slush pile? Again, no. Therefore, it's a few extraneous words that are easy to cut…and more word count you can devote to your pitch.

Similar statements fall in the too-much-information category—TMI because they are probably working against you in ways you don't realize.

The worst offender, in my opinion, is, "I wrote this book to teach readers/help readers learn..." It doesn't matter how you finish that sentence. My red flag is already rising because you've revealed that your intent is to teach. If you write nonfiction, no problem. But in the world of fiction, your number-one job is to entertain. The transactional nature of fiction is that readers give you their money hoping that in return you'll give them a few hours of worthwhile escape from the familiar. If you wrote your book with pedagogical intent, your book will risk coming across as teachy or preachy. In a teachy-preachy stories, dramatic situations are contrived and overblown, solutions are oversimplified, morality is black and white, and dialogue is trite.

Where I tend to see this most is in middle-grade and young-adult submissions. Yet the irony here—and I'm speaking to you now as a former teacher of junior-high language arts with a degree in secondary education—is that kids are smart. They can sniff a morality tale a mile away, and they don't much care for condescension. In addition, they're more capable than many adults give them credit for of understanding the complexities of the human condition. Many comprehend nuance, subtlety, and contradiction just fine, and those who don't...wait for it...*learn by reading*. So if you want to write books that challenge and develop young minds, then strive to write deep, immersive, emotionally complex stories that don't offer easy answers or on-the-nose life lessons.

A slightly altered version of this claim is "readers of my novel will learn…" The truth is—and this is something established writers already know—writers have no idea what readers of their novels will learn. If you're part of a book club, then you know all too well how six or seven people who read the same novel will report six or seven completely different experiences, impressions, levels of emotional investment, and takeaways. Once your novel is published, you'll have not just six or seven readers, but thousands (hopefully more). That means there will be thousands of different reactions to it. So it's impossible to know, and a waste of time to guess, what, if anything, readers of your novel will learn.

Other statements that may work against you, and that you'd be better off cutting from your query, include things like, "This is my fifty-seventh novel, but I'm still waiting for my first publishing deal" or "I've been writing every day for thirty years and querying for twenty-nine, and I still haven't gotten an agent." Hats off to these writers for their prolificacy and persistence, but fifty-seven unpublished novels? Thirty years? Yikes. It's difficult not to assume these are writers who aren't improving. Are they getting feedback? From whom? And more importantly, are they *listening* to it? Acting on it?

If you're a writer who's active in any sort of writing-related social-media community, you've no doubt seen tons of writers posting about their daily word count. Good for them. But if you're a slower writer, ignore those posts. Scroll right on past. Other writers' daily word-count posts are head trash that has nothing to do with you or your writing process.

Daily word counts are laudable only insofar as the writers who post them set a goal for themselves and achieved it. That means these posts are habit related, not quality related. At the end of the day—actually, at the end of your manuscript—you're better off having written a couple hundred words of well-crafted prose per day than you are having banged out a couple thousand sloppy words that readers won't be able to follow.

There's a caveat, of course. Banging out a couple thousand "don't think, just write" words a day is part of the process for a great many writers—but those are writers *who plan to revise*. Theirs is the "write hot, revise cold" approach, and it's totally legit. But I can guarantee you that Mx. Fifty-Seven Unpublished Novels isn't doing a whole lot of revising. And I'm betting that if they're getting help or advice, they're not heeding it.

Remember: Writing is different from skills like roller skating, rock climbing, or hula hooping, where the number of hours you devote to practicing *even in isolation* correlates to at least some inevitable degree of improvement. Writing is harder because reading is cerebral. It's a meaning-making phenomenon that starts in the writer's brain and ends in the reader's. *The reader is part of the process.*

In that way, writing is more akin to professional cooking, where success lies in getting the greatest possible number of people to enjoy the unique way you put flavors together and to keep coming back for more. As a writer, you're only ever doing half the work. The other half happens in readers' brains, and how well you've done your job affects how well they can do theirs. So while a roller skater, rock climber, or hula hooper doesn't need to rely on their audience's mental, emotional, and cultural intelligence, life experiences, or imaginativeness to gauge whether they've turned in an impressive performance, a writer does.

Throwing down a hefty daily word count without also soliciting and acting on feedback from teachers, editors, mentors, critique partners, or beta readers is not much different from an aspiring pianist plunking out two-thousand repetitions of middle-C every day and thinking they're somehow closer to performing Rachmaninov. Writers who don't have such folks available to them still have access to the best teachers in the world: other writers. Writers become better writers by reading, by evaluating which writers and stories they like, which they don't, and why. Reading is how you shut off the writing part of your brain for a while and practice doing the other half of the work that is story creation. Being a well-rounded storysmith means honing both skills.

Agent Kristin Nelson recently polled her clients to find out how many manuscripts they finished before they finally sold their first novel. The average was four. If you're already past that, take heart. Four was the average. But if you're *well* beyond that number and still haven't had a nibble, then evaluate whether you could benefit from reading a few bestsellers in your genre as well as from letting others read your writing and give you some feedback.

Another sentiment you'd do well to avoid is, "I wrote this novel because I was working through a difficult time in my life, and I hope it will help others who've experienced similar difficulties."

Writing, any type of writing (in fact, any type of artistic creation), is excellent therapy. It just is. But this type of disclosure in a query letter for a novel begins to raise my red flag. A writer who claims to have written a novel for self-help purposes might be climbing the wrong mountain. I might take a ballet class to alleviate stress, but that doesn't mean I'm ready to dance *Swan Lake*. It'll be years before I'm even ready for toe shoes! How long has this writer been working to master the various aspects of fiction craft—character development, voice, plot, pacing, structure, dialogue, description, mechanics, etc., etc., etc.? Long enough to make their submission competitive in the fiction-publishing market? Or is this truly a freshman effort written in response to a particular personal trauma, and as such, likely won't have the chops to stand out in a crowded and highly competitive market?

If a writer who's had seven novels published by Penguin Random House says she wrote this new project in response to a challenging time in her life, that's different. The words "seven published novels" will most likely appear in the bio as well, letting me know she's an experienced writer and veteran of the publishing process. For me, that level of experience will trump any concern I have that the submission was written solely as therapy rather than as entertainment or escape for a wide readership.

Those newer to writing who came to the page to work through real-life challenges or traumas might consider exploring memoir rather than fiction. Memoir isn't that different from fiction; both forms are built from the same elements of story craft, making memoir a more closely related cousin to the novel than to autobiography. The contract a memoirist makes with their reader is that the book will be a structured like a novel—complete with a focused story space, voice, some inciting incident, rising action, stakes, twists, etc.—but that it will also be true. The people in it really lived. The events really occurred.

Several of my query-writing workshops have attracted good mixes of memoirists and fiction writers. When it comes time to workshop students' query pitches, it's often the memoirists who are the hardest to pull details out of—details about the complete work we need in order to help them beef up and fine tune their pitches. A reticent memoirist might seem counterintuitive, but it actually makes sense. One huge challenge of writing memoir is balancing how much about oneself to reveal with how much to keep private. Memoirists owe the reader a true story, which means being vulnerable and possibly compromising the privacy of loved ones. That's not something humans are immediately comfortable with, so newer memoirists err on the side of privacy. I even heard one memoirist respond to deepening questions about the subject of her work with, "That's none of your business!" Which actually elicited a giggle and some really good follow-up discussion. But this means memoirists' first attempts at query pitches tend to be vague and hazy, and their hedging is often met with, "Well, if you don't want to tell us more, then why are you writing memoir?"

This in itself might be the reason people choose fiction when they want to write their way through a real-life challenge or trauma. Fiction is safe. It distances the writer not only from what happened to them, but also from the text itself. It allows them to explore better solutions, to imagine alternate endings.

I don't doubt that plenty of fantastic fiction was born this way. After all, all writing is steeped in the writer's thoughts, feelings, opinions, interests, and imaginations, which are formed by that magical blend of nature and nurture. But if you are writing fiction, own that you are writing fiction, and *pitch it as fiction*, not as the product of therapy or self-help, and definitely not as something you hope will help others. Remember, fiction written to *teach* can come across as stilted; fiction written to *help* can, too.

In fiction, be true to your characters and their stories, and trust that if you've done that well, then readers will find something in your work to connect to.

CHAPTER 9

IT'S TIME TO QUERY

ONCE YOU HAVE CRAFTED YOUR BEST POSSIBLE QUERY letter—from greeting and project summary to pitch and bio—and you've created your targeted list of agents to send it to, you're ready to begin. But don't make the mistake of thinking this is the time for you to sit back and wait for the offers to roll in. You still have work to do!

SET UP A TRACKING SYSTEM

Task one is to create a system for tracking your query activity. I'm a spreadsheet girl, so my advice would be to create one of those. Columns would be as follows:

- Date of submission
- Agent name
- Agent contact info. It doesn't hurt to keep the

method you used to contact each agent in one place, whether it's their email address, the email address of their assistant, the URL of their online submission form, or something else.

- Agent response time. Some agents list their typical query-response time on their websites. Here at Nelson, we respond to queries within two to three weeks, and we say so on our website. Some agents, however, don't say how long they might take with your query, so for those entries, you'd leave this field blank.
- Follow-up date. Based on your date of submission and agent response time, enter a date when, if you haven't already received a response, you will follow up on the status of your query. For agents who don't give a response time, set this date six to eight weeks from your submission date. For agents whose websites say, "Don't follow up with me about your query," do not enter a follow-up date.
- Materials sent. What you send should be what the agent says on their website that they want you to send. Query only? Query plus first ten pages? Query plus first three chapters? Whatever it is, note here that that's indeed what you sent. In addition, I'd recommend that you set up a

submissions folder somewhere on your computer. Inside this folder would be more folders, each named for one agent you submitted to. Inside each agent's folder, save a copy of the materials you sent them. We get no small number of follow-up queries from authors who are worried they sent us the wrong version of their sample pages. And I get it—all writing projects end up being one of eighteen Word docs titled final.doc, finalfinal.doc, realfinalfinal.doc, seriouslythisisthefinal.doc, and so on. But if you create electronic copies of exactly what you sent each agent *as you hit send* on each submission, you'll know. Sure, you could set up folders for all this in your email account, but remember that not all agents accept queries via email—a lot, like us, use QueryManager. So to have all your query efforts saved in one place, this electronic filing system is what I'd recommend.

- Date response received
- Response. There are more options here than *no thank you* or *please send more.* Honestly, one of the two is what you should expect; however, if an agent was on the fence about your submission, they might offer up a bit of an explanation. They might say something like, "Wow, this one was tough for me, and here's why." Whenever an agent

responds with specific feedback for you, that's good news, even if it they ultimately decline to request your full. You've probably gathered by now that agents have to move pretty quickly through their queries in order to keep up, so specific, personalized feedback, even if only a sentence or two, means your submission gave them pause. They thought hard about it and took the time to let you know instead of sending you their canned query rejection. Sometimes their feedback might be related to timing or the current market, like, "This is a strong submission and you're a talented writer, but Trope X is a tough sell right now," or, "I wish you'd sent this to me a year ago!"

Personalized, as opposed to canned, query rejections might end with the agent inviting you to query them for something different. So the response column is where you'd enter one of the following: *send full, send sample pages, pass, pass with personalized comment*, or *pass with invitation to submit something different.*

- Date requested materials sent. From here on out, these additional columns are only necessary for tracking requests for sample pages or your full manuscript.
- Follow-up date. Set a date to follow up on your requested materials. The agent's website might say

how long you should wait to follow up on sample pages or full manuscripts. If it doesn't, you're probably safe to set a date six to eight weeks out on sample pages, and ten to twelve weeks out on a full.

- Date of response.
- Response. Similar to query responses, the responses you might get after an agent has read your full manuscript could be an offer of representation (time to celebrate!), a pass, a pass with an invitation to submit a different project, or a revise-and-resubmit—an R&R, in industry speak.

We'll talk more about R&Rs and how to approach them in a bit. But first, after you have your tracking spreadsheet set up, there's one more important thing to consider.

QUERY STRATEGY

Here's a question I get a lot when I teach query workshops or speak at conferences: Once I have my list of agents ready, what do I do? Query them all at once or query a few at a time?

There's no perfect answer to this. Every strategy has its pros and cons.

You certainly could query every agent on your list

all at once. But some writers who've been at the query game awhile will tell you why they prefer not to do it that way. Their hope is that if they query a few agents at a time and then wait for responses, they might get some personalized feedback along with their rejections that they can use to strengthen their submission before they send it out to the next wave.

That's solid advice, and while it might preclude your sending a flawed submission to everyone all at once, it does slow things down for you quite a bit.

Another strategy is to divide your agent list into your A, B, and C agents, the A's being your top-level, dream agents. Then the question becomes, do you query your A's or C's first?

Again, those who would advise you to start with your C's and then move on to your B's argue that you'll have the opportunity to improve your submission before sending it to your A's. But what if you get offers from your C or B agents? Then you have to scramble to submit to your A's with an offer already on the table, which can be a weird submission to receive. (If you wanted to work with us, then why did you wait to query us until after you had an offer from someone else?)

On the other hand, you could start with your A's and work your way to your C's. That way, if you get an offer from an A-level agent, then you've saved yourself the trouble of querying the ones who were never as high a priority for you to begin with.

There's a certain prestige that comes with multiple offers. Agents understand that. The more offers, the greater the prestige, it seems, especially among writers whose offers are coming in through high-profile pitch contests or mentorship programs. If you're ever in the enviable position of entertaining four, eight, ten offers, even more, please only solicit additional interest from agents you really want to work with. Every agent who catches wind that there's a hot manuscript making the rounds will drop everything to read it, so your casting a wide net at that point just to inflate your total number of offers isn't respectful of their time.

Whatever your strategy, don't stress too much about it. The important thing is that you've written the best possible book, you've crafted the best possible query letter, and you're sending it to a targeted list of agents who, based on your research, would be most likely to represent it.

HOW TO HANDLE AN R&R

A revise-and-resubmit, or R&R, means the agent suggests specific revisions and asks you to resubmit your manuscript if you decide to make those revisions. An R&R is not an offer of rep, so you are under no obligation to make their suggested revisions (it's your book, after all), and they are under no obligation to sign you if you do. Know that in-depth R&Rs are risky for agents because the author might revise accordingly, and then submit the stronger work to a different agent. For that reason, and because a meaningful R&R is no small amount of work for an agent to pull together, R&Rs are not particularly common.

Know also that six different agents who read your full will most likely have six different ideas about how you should revise it. Getting six passes on your manuscript for six different reasons can be incredibly frustrating—at least if they all had the same reason for passing, you'd know how to revise the darn thing!

But just as frustrating would be getting six R&Rs. Which agent's editorial suggestions do you act on, especially knowing that afterward, none of those agents is obligated to offer you rep? The easy answer is, the suggestions that will require you to do the least amount of work, obviously! But few things in this industry are easy, so easy should be suspect. Instead, really dive deep into which suggestions resonate with you. Which R&R makes you think, "Dang, I wish I'd thought of that." Don't get too hung up on rejecting fantastic ideas just because they weren't your own. The further on you get in your career as Professional Writer, the more you'll come to realize that most bestsellers were team efforts. Really good agents and really good editors get really good books out of their authors. So don't shy away from a big revision.

I know two writers who each received more than one R&R and executed multiple revisions to see which one would net an offer. Neither cared which agent they got an offer from; they were doing the work that would increase their odds of getting representation. That's certainly something you could do, if you have the time and energy to write multiple versions of your novel. You'll only know later, in hindsight, whether it was a good strategy.

In any case, start a new document where you collect any and all personalized feedback or R&R notes you get from the agents you queried. Collecting this feedback in one place allows you to see patterns emerge. If more than one agent commented that they couldn't connect with your main character or that they found her unsympathetic or unlikable, that should be something you give due consideration. If more than one agent commented that they were confused when your characters started time traveling at your manuscript's 60,000-word mark, that's a plot point you might want to rethink.

RESPONDING TO REJECTIONS

When you receive rejections (and you *will* receive rejections, and that is OK—it's part of the process), it's best not to respond. It might surprise you to learn that agents receive angry, aggressive, even threatening responses to form rejections all the time. Or maybe it doesn't surprise you. In any case, it's horrifying, even if we know on a logical level that such things aren't personal.

Less horrifying are the responses we receive from writers who want to somehow invalidate their rejection. For instance, one writer recently responded to our form rejection by "correcting" a grammatical error in it (he was incorrect). His tone was so condescending that his intent was obvious: to knock us down a peg so that the idea of *us* rejecting *him* was easier for him to swallow. And Agent Kristin recently received a letter via snail mail from an author she had sent a rejection to *twelve years earlier*. This author had just received her first publishing contract, and she wanted Kristin to know that she was wrong to have rejected her all those years ago.

Some writers respond to rejections to solicit a reason for why their work was rejected. Where did their submission go wrong, and what can they do to make it better? I wish we had the time to give constructive feedback to everyone who queries us, or even to everyone who asks, but that's just not realistic. The good news for all writers, though, is that so many other resources are available to them. I've mentioned many before, but I'll mention them again: in-person and online critique groups, in-person and online workshops, beta readers, critiques through writing conferences and contests, live slush-pile panels at conferences, freelance editors, manuscript swaps (you critique my manuscript, I'll critique yours), and mentorship programs. Seek feedback, learning, and advice through those channels not only before you query, but also long after you've become established in your writing career. Plenty of our bestselling author-clients still meet regularly with their critique groups to brainstorm, swap chapters, troubleshoot sticky scenes or plots, and so on. Know now that the learning never stops.

Maybe you just want to send a nice response thanking the agent for their time. That's a nice sentiment, but it's wholly unnecessary. However, if it's clear that the rejection you received is not the agent's form rejection—that is, they provided specific feedback, calling out your characters by name, referencing particular events or plot points in your manuscript—then the agent took more time with your submission than they do with most others. At that point, a nice "thank you" can be nice to hear, but it's certainly neither required nor expected.

RE-QUERYING PREVIOUSLY REJECTED MANUSCRIPTS

Some agents are quite clear: If they've rejected your submission once, they're not interested in seeing it again, even if you revise it. So unless such agents specifically issued you an R&R, if they passed, then take them off your query list for this project.

That doesn't mean you can't query them for a different manuscript. And you don't need to reply to a rejection for Manuscript A with an email asking if it's OK to submit a query for Manuscript B. If Manuscript B is still appropriate for the agent's list, then when it's ready, just do it.

In addition, don't reply to a rejection for Manuscript A with an email asking if the agent would consider looking at a revision in a few weeks or months. Their answer will be no, because their reasons for rejecting you are still fresh in their mind. It's better to just do the revision and (don't tell anyone I advised you to do this) submit it again later. How much later? I'd say no sooner than six months.

When you do resubmit, do not open your query with, "You rejected this before, but I've done a significant revision, so I'm hoping…" That's not leading with your strengths! Instead, in the interest of disclosure, mention at the end of your query letter that the manuscript has recently been revised—better yet, recently revised with the help of so-and-so freelance editor, recently revised after you attended a critique session with so-and-so bestselling author, recently revised after you participated in a workshop with so-and-so story doctor, recently revised with help from so-and-so mentor, or recently revised per an R&R you received from another agent (if any one of these secenarios is the case).

This way, your new query letter—which you'll of course have reworked so that it's up-to-date and so that the pitch is appropriate to the revised manuscript—will get a fresh read. If the agent gets into your pitch and thinks, "This sounds familiar," then your disclosure at the end will explain why. But hopefully you'll have hooked them with this shiny new version of your submission, and they just might be enticed enough to go ahead and request your revised manuscript.

I should note, however, that agents who use Query-Manager (and perhaps other web-based submission-management systems that I'm not familiar with) can see at a glance your entire history of contacting their agency. QM flags duplicate submissions based on title, author name, author email, and even the IP address of the computer the author used to send their submission—and it does so across all agents who work for the same agency. That means if you query Agent A in April and Agent A rejects you in May, and then you query Agent B in June, your submission to Agent B will come in flagged as a duplicate. Agent B can see your April submission to Agent A plus all messages you and Agent A may have exchanged through QM about your submission.

Again, the cross-visibility only works for agents

within the same agency, but be aware that it's a thing. We expressly ask on our website that authors query only one of our agents at a time, so it's immediately obvious on our end when an author didn't follow that instruction. Such queries come in flagged as duplicates.

If I open a new query for one of our agents and see that a duplicate was received six months prior, I as the slush reader will click back and forth to compare the two submissions and evaluate how much of a revision has been done. If the two subs are substantially similar, the new one will be a quick pass. If, however, it's clear the author has revised, I will read the submission with a fresh eye.

HOW TO HANDLE AN OFFER OF REPRESENTATION

In the best possible world, every agent you queried will offer you rep. That's not realistic, but one can dream! It's not out of the ordinary, however, for an author to receive more than one offer. If that's you, here's what to do.

When the first offer comes in, be sure to have a phone call with that agent. That phone call can be enough to help you evaluate whether you would be a good professional team. If it's awkward or weird in any way, then you might not be the best professional fit for each other.

If this is your dream agent, the one who has been at the top of your list all along and you can't imagine entertaining an offer from anyone else, then accept the offer. Immediately contact all the other agents you queried, thank them for their time, and withdraw your submission.

If, however, you would entertain offers from other agents, then ask the agent who issued your first offer to give you two weeks to decide. This is standard. They will be expecting this. If they pressure you to sign with them earlier than that, be extremely wary.

Next, look at the other agents from whom you are still waiting for a response. If some of them are now low on your list, contact them and withdraw your submission. Let them off the hook. Then message all the other agents immediately to say you have received an offer of representation and that you will be making a decision by a specific date. Don't just say *in two weeks*; look at your calendar and figure out which date is two weeks from the date of your offer from Agent 1.

Some offer-of-rep notifications are too perfunctory: "I have an offer. You have two weeks to get back to me." Yikes. That sounds like a hostage negotiation, not a professional communication. You can do better! You don't have to disclose who offered you rep, though some agents will ask (mostly because they want to make sure you're not fibbing about having an offer, which no small number of writers do if they think it will shuffle their submission to the top of everyone's pile), so it doesn't hurt you to disclose this.

It's possible over the next two weeks that another offer or two might come in. It's likely you'll get some passes, too. But as your deadline approaches, it's up to you to talk to each of the agents who've thrown their hats in your ring to decide which offer you want to accept. Most importantly, don't feel obligated to sign with the first agent who offered. They might not be the best fit, nor the best option for launching the career you want. For a list of questions to ask and a more in-depth look at what to watch out for in an agency contract, check out my book *Do You Need a Literary Agent?*

MOVING ON TO YOUR NEXT PROJECT

Throughout this process, I can't overstate the importance of continuing to write. Don't make the mistake of putting a halt to your writing efforts, thinking you'll get back to writing once this particular manuscript sells. Get to work on your next book, whether it's a sequel or something completely different.

Whatever your path to representation looks like—and beyond that, your journey to publication and your status as Professional Writer—I sincerely hope this book was part of getting you that *yes* you were looking for. All it takes is one *yes*, and you'll be on your way.

APPENDIX

RECOMMENDED RESOURCES

James Scott Bell • *Plot and Structure: Techniques and Exercises for Crafting a Plot that Grips Readers from Start to Finish*

James Scott Bell • *Revision and Self-Editing: Techniques for Transforming Your First Draft into a Finished Novel*

James Scott Bell • *Write Your Novel from the Middle: A New Approach for Plotters, Pantsers, and Everyone in Between*

Jessica Brody • *Save the Cat! Writes a Novel: The Last Book on Novel Writing You'll Ever Need*

Larry Brooks • *Story Engineering: Mastering the 6 Core Competencies of Successful Writing*

Larry Brooks • *Great Stories Don't Write Themselves: Criteria-Driven Strategies for More Effective Fiction*

Lisa Cron • *Story Genius: How to Use Brain Science to Go Beyond Outlining and Write a Riveting Novel (Before You Waste Three Years Writing 327 Pages That Go Nowhere)*

Lisa Cron • *Wired for Story: The Writer's Guide to Using Brain Science to Hook Readers from the Very First Sentence*

David Farland • *Million Dollar Outlines*

John Gardner • *The Art of Fiction: Notes on Craft for Young Writers*

Ursula K. Le Guin • *Steering the Craft: A Twenty-First Century Guide to Sailing the Sea of Story*

Francine Prose • *Reading Like a Writer: A Guide for People Who Love Books and for Those Who Want to Write Them*

Jeffrey Alan Schechter • *My Story Can Beat Up Your Story: Ten Ways to Toughen Up Your Screenplay from Opening Hook to Knockout Punch*

John Truby • *The Anatomy of Story: 22 Steps to Becoming a Master Storyteller*

Christopher Vogler • *The Writer's Journey: Mythical Structure for Writers*

ABOUT THE AUTHOR

Angie Hodapp is the Director of Literary Development at Nelson Literary Agency. A graduate of the Publishing Institute at the University of Denver, she holds a BA in English education and an MA in English with an emphasis in communication development. She has worked in language education and professional writing and editing for more than twenty years and is a frequent presenter at writing conferences and literary events. Dedicated to helping writers improve their craft and learn about the ever-changing publishing industry, Angie is the author of the Writer-in-the-Know series.

Made in the USA
Coppell, TX
17 October 2023